MOTIVATIONAL INTERVIEWING IN SCHOOLS

Applications of Motivational Interviewing

Stephen Rollnick, William R. Miller,
and Theresa B. Moyers, *Series Editors*
www.guilford.com/AMI

Since the publication of Miller and Rollnick's classic *Motivational Interviewing*, now in its third edition, MI has been widely adopted as a tool for facilitating change. This highly practical series includes general MI resources as well as books on specific clinical contexts, problems, and populations. Each volume presents powerful MI strategies that are grounded in research and illustrated with concrete, "how-to-do-it" examples.

Motivational Interviewing in Health Care:
Helping Patients Change Behavior
Stephen Rollnick, William R. Miller, and Christopher C. Butler

Building Motivational Interviewing Skills: A Practitioner Workbook
David B. Rosengren

Motivational Interviewing with Adolescents and Young Adults
Sylvie Naar-King and Mariann Suarez

Motivational Interviewing in Social Work Practice
Melinda Hohman

Motivational Interviewing in the Treatment of Anxiety
Henny A. Westra

Motivational Interviewing, Third Edition: Helping People Change
William R. Miller and Stephen Rollnick

Motivational Interviewing in Groups
Christopher C. Wagner and Karen S. Ingersoll, with Contributors

Motivational Interviewing in the Treatment
of Psychological Problems, Second Edition
Hal Arkowitz, William R. Miller, and Stephen Rollnick, Editors

Motivational Interviewing in Diabetes Care
Marc P. Steinberg and William R. Miller

Motivational Interviewing in Nutrition and Fitness
Dawn Clifford and Laura Curtis

Motivational Interviewing in Schools:
Conversations to Improve Behavior and Learning
Stephen Rollnick, Sebastian G. Kaplan, and Richard Rutschman

Motivational Interviewing in Schools

Conversations to Improve Behavior and Learning

STEPHEN ROLLNICK
SEBASTIAN G. KAPLAN
RICHARD RUTSCHMAN

THE GUILFORD PRESS
New York   London

Copyright © 2016 The Guilford Press
A Division of Guilford Publications, Inc.
370 Seventh Avenue, Suite 1200, New York, NY 10001
www.guilford.com

Printed in the United States of America

This book is printed on acid-free paper.

Last digit is print number: 9 8 7 6 5 4 3 2

The authors have checked with sources believed to be reliable in their efforts to provide
information that is complete and generally in accord with the standards of practice that
are accepted at the time of publication. However, in view of the possibility of human error
or changes in behavioral, mental health, or medical sciences, neither the authors, nor
the editor and publisher, nor any other party who has been involved in the preparation
or publication of this work warrants that the information contained herein is in every
respect accurate or complete, and they are not responsible for any errors or omissions
or the results obtained from the use of such information. Readers are encouraged to
confirm the information contained in this book with other sources.

Library of Congress Cataloging-in-Publication Data

Names: Rollnick, Stephen, 1952- author.
Title: Motivational interviewing in schools : conversations to improve
    behavior and learning / Stephen Rollnick, Sebastian G. Kaplan, Richard
    Rutschman.
Description: New York : The Guilford Press, 2016. | Series: Applications of
    motivational interviewing | Includes bibliographical references and index.
Identifiers: LCCN 2016027079 | ISBN 9781462527274 (paperback) |
    ISBN 9781462527281 (hardcover)
Subjects: LCSH: Teacher participation in educational counseling. |
    Motivational interviewing. | BISAC: PSYCHOLOGY / Psychotherapy / Child &
    Adolescent. | SOCIAL SCIENCE / Social Work. | EDUCATION / Counseling /
    General.
Classification: LCC LB1027.5 .R588 2016 | DDC 371.4/046--dc23
LC record available at https://lccn.loc.gov/2016027079

For Maya, Stefan, Jake, Nina,
and our little big boy, Nathan Albie
—S. R.

For Sarah, Cole, Jordan, and Brennan
—S. G. K.

For my parents and Peg, Luke, Jesse,
Elijah, Lou, and Micah
—R. R.

About the Authors

Stephen Rollnick, PhD, is Honorary Distinguished Professor at the Cochrane Institute of Primary Care and Public Health at Cardiff University, United Kingdom. A clinical psychologist with many years of experience and a codeveloper of motivational interviewing (MI), as well as a cofounder of the Motivational Interviewing Network of Trainers (MINT), Dr. Rollnick provides consultancy and training on the subjects of motivation, change, and MI. His research and guidelines for good practice have been widely published, and his work on implementation continues, with a current focus on children with HIV/AIDS in Africa, pregnant teens in deprived communities, and MI for teachers and sports coaches.

Sebastian G. Kaplan, PhD, is a clinical psychologist and Associate Professor in the Department of Psychiatry and Behavioral Medicine, Child and Adolescent Psychiatry Section, at the Wake Forest University School of Medicine. A former special education teacher, Dr. Kaplan currently focuses his clinical work on helping adolescents and their families overcome a variety of challenges to their growth and development. He has written and presented on the application of MI for pediatricians, mental health providers, and school personnel, and is a member of MINT.

Richard Rutschman, EdD, is Senior Program Manager and Professional Development Facilitator at the Center for College Access and

Success (formerly the Chicago Teachers' Center) at Northeastern Illinois University. His professional experience in Chicago schools has included being a high school science and Spanish teacher and the principal of an alternative high school. Throughout his career, he has worked to support school improvement efforts focusing on student retention, engagement, leadership development, and preparation for postsecondary education. Dr. Rutschman is a recipient of the Michael Stratton Practitioner Award from the International Association for Experiential Education for his work using adventure initiatives in Chicago schools, and is a member of MINT.

Preface

This book has a single aim: to improve everyday conversations about change in schools, so that there is less struggle and more enjoyment of life and learning for students, teachers, and other school staff. Our focus is any conversation with students that helps them to be more motivated to change their attitudes and behaviors, like getting better grades, feeling happier in school, being less disruptive, getting on better with peers and teachers, and so on. We also are interested in conversations about chronic student lateness, disruptive classroom behavior, mental health, heated student conflicts, unmotivated students, and any student problem where the use of consequences might fail. These conversations take place in routine exchanges, sometimes in heated ones about very difficult behavior, and sometimes in those quieter moments when a student is struggling with new learning.

The book's focus on everyday conversations is an attempt to bring a set of skills called "motivational interviewing" (MI) into a world where connecting with students is a challenge for all involved. *It is written not just for teachers, but for all those who work behind them: administrators, counselors, tutors, social workers, parents, advocates, and all support staff.* The book is about what you say, and how you say it, the front end of relationship building that we believe lies at the heart of good education.

Do conversations promote change? The style you use and the way you conduct the conversation seem to matter. That's where MI comes in. It is a conversation style developed in health and social care where change is often a priority. It has been refined and evaluated in research studies over more than 30 years, with a special focus on situations where someone is in conflict or is uncertain about change—hence the use of "motivational" in its name.

MI does not need to focus only on problems. It can be used to help people clarify what is important to them, where their strengths lie, and how change might come about. Although fairly new in schools, it clearly shares a common goal with education: to help students to grow and change. The impetus for writing the book comes from the need to work with students' strengths alongside whatever struggles they are having.

Finally, we hope this book might prove to be a catalyst for a culture change in education that champions authentic relationships as the vehicle for all that follows. In this sense, we hope MI might play its part as an expression of this core value in education.

A Word about Us

We hope that as you read this book it becomes evident that we are passionate about education, and enthusiastic about the potential for MI to be of use to teachers and others who work in schools every day. We have traversed varied paths en route to using and writing about MI.

SR: I am one of the cofounders of MI, and it took a deputy principal to pull me into the world of education. He came up to me during a training workshop and said, "We want to improve relationships all 'round, and I'm here to improve my skills. I think MI could be very important. Can you come and visit us?" What I saw and heard on visiting his school was the fuel for writing this book. Small moments that mattered were scattered across the classrooms and corridors, so different from my own experience as a student, often in trouble. I would have thrived in that school. Then I started working with my coauthors, and those conversations lifted our motivation to see if we could help schools to cherish and champion what is already within their grasp: conversations that help to change lives.

SGK: During my final year in college, I completed an internship at an elementary school in Amherst, Massachusetts, supporting the inclusion of students with special needs into a fifth-grade classroom. I had the great fortune of working with a fantastic lead teacher, Alice Goodwin-Brown (aka Ms. G-B). I still remember my first meeting with her as we discussed my "caseload." As we came upon one student in particular, a young boy with a lengthy list of behavioral and academic challenges, the first words out of Ms. G-B's mouth were, "I just love that kid," and she proceeded to describe all of his wonderful qualities. I was struck by her words that day, and by the genuine caring she exhibited every day with all of her students. As I evolved in my early career, both as a teacher of students with special needs and as a basketball coach, I strived to uphold this quality that Ms. G-B so artfully expressed: to keep the strengths in all my students and players front and center. My first encounter with MI occurred late in my psychology training, when a supervisor of mine mentioned the approach as a way to curiously explore challenges with people, without judgment or confrontation. This felt quite familiar to me given what I had learned from Ms. G-B's strengths-based teaching style.

RR: I have been working with vulnerable students for nearly four decades in the role of advocate, teacher, high school principal, executive director, and higher education administrator of school improvement partnerships. After college, I volunteered with the Alternative Schools Network in Chicago as a youth advocate and high school teacher with gang-involved youth and dropouts. I had frequent conversations with young people, seeking to get them to change. While creating programs that gave them a sense of belonging helped, too often these students experienced incarceration or tragically lost their lives to gun violence. Undoubtedly, they knew I was concerned and cared about them, but my concern seldom seemed to lead them to change. Over the years, I looked for approaches for supporting marginalized, at-risk youth to help them get on track. When I discovered MI from my wife, a nurse and public health professional, I was intrigued. As I learned more about MI and used it with students, it became clear to me that this was an approach I would have valued in the past.

Acknowledgments

There are people, stories, and experiences too personal and too numerous to mention that helped us to write this book. However, a few people stand out like lighthouses. We wish to thank Andy Williams from Monmouth Comprehensive School in Wales, who absorbed motivational interviewing (MI) as easily as he opened up the doors of his wonderful school. Danny Gordon and Robert Valle from Northeastern Illinois University's Center for College Access and Success deserve congratulations for seeing the value in and experimenting with MI, as does the center's leader, Wendy Stack, for supporting the training of teachers, staff, mentors, parent advocates, and graduate students in Chicago schools. Members of the Motivational Interviewing Network of Trainers freely gave time, wisdom, and advice to us for many years. Sincere thanks are extended to our spouses, Nina Gobat, Sarah Kaplan, and Peg Dublin for their patience and support, including serving as sounding boards and reviewing first drafts.

The team of Series Editor William R. Miller, Senior Editor Jim Nageotte, and developmental editor Barbara Watkins, of The Guilford Press, tore into earlier drafts like tigers. We sweated, and can only thank them for such meticulous attention to clarity and much more.

Then, in the distant past, there was a teacher who made a big difference. Thank you.

Contents

PART I. OVERVIEW OF MOTIVATIONAL INTERVIEWING   1

1. Conversations about Change   3

2. What Is MI?   11

3. The Spirit and Style of MI   20

4. A Conversation Map: Four Processes   27

5. Core Skills   33

6. Evoking: The Heart of MI   44

7. Planning Changes   54

8. The MI Approach to Giving Information and Advice   62

PART II. IN PRACTICE   69

9. Behavior, Behavior, Behavior   73

10. Learning   87

11. Personal Growth   102

12. Working with Families   116

PART III. FOCUSED APPLICATIONS   129

13. Bullying   131

14. At-Risk Students: MI Integrated   139
     with Other Approaches

15. Dropout Prevention and Reengagement   146

16. Transition to Life after School   158

PART IV. BROADER HORIZONS   167

17. Improving Your Knowledge and Skills   169

18. Integrating MI in Schools   191

References   205

Index   215

Additional resources for learning and practicing MI,
including sample agendas and ideas for introductory
presentations to educators, are available at
www.guilford.com/rollnick2-materials.

MOTIVATIONAL INTERVIEWING IN SCHOOLS

OVERVIEW OF MOTIVATIONAL INTERVIEWING

This book is structured so as to provide an overview of motivational interviewing (MI) (Part I), worked examples of everyday applications (Part II), discussion of challenges like bullying and at-risk students (Part III) and finally, attention to learning MI and wider integration (Part IV).

The eight chapters in this first part all use examples from school life to illustrate how MI might be used in that setting. There's a critical question—"*Why MI?*"—which is where we start (Chapter 1). Chapter 2 is probably best to read before any of those that follow in Part I because it provides an overview with signposts to the next six chapters, each of which tackles a different topic.

Uniting all the chapters in Part I is a single thread that should be of interest to those working in schools: your conversation skills matter a great deal, as an expression of your and the school's values, and as a vehicle for promoting change. MI is designed to sharpen your skills to the benefit of both you and your students.

1

Conversations about Change

> It really all depends on how the teachers and
> students interact.
>
> —*A student, in answer to the question
> "What is a good school?"*

Motivational interviewing (MI) focuses on improving motivation to change, and it does this through conversation. This book is about how the conversation skills you already have can be refined to inspire change in classrooms, corridors, and cafeterias. It's about how to improve student motivation, behavior and growth.[1] It's also about how you can enjoy your conversations, be more efficient, conserve your energy, and have a greater impact. In the end, it's about how well-known principles of good education can be realized through more effective conversation.

Attending to student behavior is no easy task. For example, in the United States, one recent year (2006) saw 7% of students suspended at least once, amounting to 3.3 million youth (Losen, 2011). In another analysis over a million students walked out of their school before graduating, never to return (Datiri, 2013). At the milder end of the spectrum, efforts to improve performance are often based on the idea that with

---

[1] This book focuses on primary and secondary schools. However, it's a fairly short step into the world of higher education. The style and techniques of MI will endure across settings even if the content of the conversations might be a little different.

sufficient pressure and reinforcement, student motivation will improve. Loud encouragement, and often coercion, is the norm.

MI offers an alternative strategy. It has been refined over the last 30 years to produce a strengths-based vehicle for you to support students in finding their own routes to change (Miller & Rollnick, 2013). It can be useful whether you are a teacher, administrator, counselor, or coach. MI offers tools for responding effectively to situations like these:

> A 9-year-old student is downhearted, struggling with a math problem and says, "I just don't get it, I never do."

> A girl of 12 ambles casually into the classroom, late again. You ask why and the reply is "Dunno."

> You are discussing progress with a 15-year-old student and her father, and he says, "This kind of performance is unacceptable. She's just not applying herself like she should."

The conversations that unfold in the above scenarios will all focus on change, whether in behavior, motivation, or learning. If you could wave a magic wand, you would make students instantly motivated and ready to change their attitudes or behavior. Instead, such change takes effort, both yours and the student's. What would you say next in each of the above conversations?

The Righting Reflex

A common response in situations like those above is to use what we call the "righting reflex." It's a well-intentioned inclination to fix the problem for the person. It works sometimes, like when a student asks for advice. It's essential too when you need to provide information, address something quickly, or when students have no choice but to follow the rules. But for lifting a student's motivation to change, it's not very successful. Here's what the righting reflex could look like in each of those three scenarios:

> The student who says, "I just don't get it, I never do" might hear something like, "If you sit down and really concentrate you will find a way to solve this, and your grade will improve."

> The girl who says "Dunno" when asked why she is late might be met with, "Well, that's twice this week and the next step will be detention, so make sure you are on time."

And the father and daughter might hear, "Have you thought about staying after school each day and going for extra help?"

Trying to lift motivation with the righting reflex takes effort and time on your part. So how do students respond? One can predict a defensive reaction, with the word "but" appearing soon, either out loud or more quietly. If the conversation were a dance, then surely some toes are being stepped on.

> *The righting reflex: an inclination to fix the problem for the student.*

Ambivalence

A student's ambivalence about change is often close to the surface of the exchanges we've been discussing. One part of the student's mind might want to change, hearing all the reasons *for* it; another part hears the opposite, reasons *against* change. Ambivalence is a very common and normal human experience, characterized by a sort of internal mental chatter: "Should I change, or keep things the same?"; "I want to"; "I'm not sure"; "I'm getting there"; "It's not worth it"; and so on, back and forth. If motivation—the incentive and enthusiasm—is the drive to do something, the voices in favor fuel it, and those against hold it back.

When the righting reflex meets with ambivalence in the student, the conversation takes an unfortunate turn. What students hear from you is the case for change, one side of the ambivalence they feel; their response is quite predictably to voice the other side, to defend the status quo. For example:

The student struggling with math might say or think, "Yes, but . . . I've tried and it never works."

The girl who is late might say, "Yes, OK," and think to herself, "I don't like this place, so why should I bother?"

And the daughter of the annoyed father might say, "But I don't want to."

It seems like the harder you try to instill motivation, the more students resist. You and the student feel stuck. It's like a dance that's going wrong, and your head hurts trying to find the next clever move.

In each of the above examples, the student is saying why change is *not* a good idea. That's a signal worth noting. It would make much more sense if the student, not you, were to make the case for change. MI is designed to do just this.

There's an inclination in all of us to provide solutions, toughen up, talk straight, or tighten disciplinary boundaries. Students, particularly those who are not doing so well, often hear this forceful language of reward and punishment. One teacher described it as a traffic light system: Green means, "Go here, yes that's right, well done, you will get good grades and do well in life," while Red means, "No, stop, don't go there, you'll get punished and . . . ." The effect on student motivation of repeatedly hearing "do this, do that" messages might well be a negative one (DeCharmes, 1968; Chirkov & Ryan, 2001; Gonzalez-DeHass, Willems, & Holbein, 2005; Valerand & Bissonnette, 1992). Put bluntly, it's very hard to instill motivation in someone else. We like a decision to change to come from within us, not from outside pressure. Children are no different. When they reply with a shrug of the shoulders, or a more strident expression of why they won't or can't change, what's next?

> *What students hear from you is the case for change, one side of the ambivalence; their response is to voice the other side.*

> *It's hard to instill motivation in someone else.*

What MI Is

MI is a style with a set of skills used to have a conversation in which the student voices the case for change, what we call "change talk." Change is more likely to occur because it comes from students as an expression of what they want or need.

Rather than hearing you make the case for change, the students hear themselves make it, and this experience makes it easier for them to resolve their ambivalence and make a decision to change. They take charge of the decision making. A new world opens up, their motivation improves, and, bit by bit, conversation by conversation, better outcomes are seen. The more you show respect for the unique potential and strengths of students to change, the more likely they will be to do just that. You will recognize this approach in the principles of student-centered teaching practice, with children of all ages. MI merely provides the conversational tools for doing this, even in very tough situations.

The energy that drives change comes from within students themselves, with you as their support and guide, working with their strengths and aspirations. MI is founded on the conviction that students *can*

> *MI is a style for having a conversation in which the student voices the case for change.*

change. This involves a shift in your conversation style, from instilling to eliciting, acting more like a guide than an instructor, and is the foundation for all that follows in this book.

Is MI easy to learn? Yes and no. The style of conversation involved can feel a little different than that you are used to. Learning requires practice. When you start to settle into the style, and feel pleased about your progress, you can find things moving quite quickly.

What MI Is Not

MI is not a panacea, but merely a way of having a constructive conversation. Forces outside of your control, like students' friendships and their home life, often hold sway over them and prevent your best efforts from having an impact. It would be unrealistic to elevate MI beyond its place, but in its place it can be a powerful tool, or, as one colleague put it, "a powerful ingredient in the fuel that drives good practice" (David Olds, personal communication).

Using MI need not be time-consuming, and it is not a form of counseling in which you passively absorb whatever someone says.

MI is not a behavior change technique, trick, or strategy done *on* or *to* students, but rather something done *with* them, or on their behalf. It's certainly not a way of getting someone to do something he or she would not otherwise want to do. It's best not viewed as a behavior management technique, but as a way of helping someone make decisions. MI is something practiced with students to help them see the paths in front of them and choose those leading to positive growth and fulfilment. It's not just for troubled students, though it will certainly help them; it's something that can and has been used to inform conversations in all corners of school life.

> *MI is practiced with students; it's not done to or on them.*

MI in Schools

The underlying style and techniques of MI can be used in a class with a group of students as well as with individuals. MI can also be adjusted to take into account the developmental age of a child. The way we relate to students of any age can affect their motivation to change. MI, with its emphasis on supporting autonomy, is certainly well suited to adolescents. It is also the case that young children, with their lively imaginations, would benefit from a warm and accepting approach that allows them to consider their own reasons for change. Guidelines for helping younger children are highlighted in Part II.

Our experience with students, and with MI in other settings like health care, is that MI crosses cultural boundaries with little difficulty. One overview of research suggests that, in the United States, it is more effective when used with minority populations, primarily Hispanic and African American communities (Hettema, Steele, & Miller, 2005).

MI is compatible with good teaching practice, where one person takes the role of helping another move from indecision to action, from feeling stuck to feeling more motivated to change.

The overlap between MI and conversations in schools are striking:

- The word "education" is derived from the Latin verb *ducere,* "to lead or guide," which points to the value of a teacher who "draws forth" learning from students. MI focuses on the conversation techniques for exactly this "drawing forth," to enhance motivation to change. We call it evoking, a refinement of what has been called a Socratic style of education.
- Experience in the classroom, supported by evidence, tells us that students learn best when they actively participate and willingly take responsibility for their own behavior and learning, supported by skillful teaching techniques. This is easier said than done. Students often seem ambivalent about participating and taking responsibility for themselves or downright opposed to the idea. MI provides the tools for encouraging participation, resolving ambivalence, and helping students to verbalize their own routes to change.
- There is solid evidence that giving students specific, accurate, and positive feedback increases motivation. "Affirmation" is a highly tuned way of doing just this and a core skill in MI.
- Respecting and encouraging autonomy is a part of MI and is supported by educational research. Students perform better on

tests, and feel more competent and motivated to learn, when teachers actively support their autonomy.

- Teachers routinely ask open questions. In MI, open questions are followed by the use of further skills like reflective listening that encourage more discussion. If open questions are like knocking on a door, the other skills help you walk inside with greater ease.

It's worth noting here that Carl Rogers, who conducted pioneering work on education, is the same person who developed client-centered counseling, upon which we based our account of MI. Listening sits at the center of Rogers's last book, *A Way of Being* (1980), and the work of some of his students, such as Thomas Gordon (2003). Understanding what listening really means, and how it can be used, is one of the main threads running through this book. Our hope is that MI will provide you with the tools you need to use listening and other skills creatively, and with a productive focus on change. Motivation to change is clearly influenced by rewards, punishment, test scores, and so on, but the internally driven aspirations of the student are powerful, and your conversations, informed by MI skills like listening, can help students to tap their aspirations.

The Evidence

The wider research literature on MI beyond the school environment includes over 200 controlled trials and evidence for efficacy in a wide range of settings (Miller & Rollnick, 2013), including successful applications with adolescents (Naar-King & Suarez, 2011). Generally, MI's school-based applications have either been student-focused, designed to directly help those with a particular change problem, or consultative, where MI is used to help an educator or parent adopt a strategy when working with a student(s) (Strait, McQuillon, Terry, & Smith, 2014). In the most recent review of MI applications among school students, Snape and Atkinson (2016) classified 8 out of 11 studies as "best evidence," 3 were randomized trials, and all but one study yielded positive findings.

Many of the studies on MI in schools have looked to improve student health. School nurses have utilized MI to address complex problems such as obesity (Bonde, Bentsen, & Hindhede, 2014) and asthma (Blaakman, Cohen, Fagnano, & Halterman, 2014), as well as to help students increase their physical activity (Robbins, Pfeiffer, Maier, LaDrig, & Berg-Smith, 2012; Robbins, Pfeiffer, Wesolek, & Lo, 2013). Studies have also shown promising outcomes when using a school-based MI approach to help students decrease drug or alcohol use (Barnett et al., 2014; Hall, Stewart, Arger, Athenour, & Effinger, 2014; Hamilton, O'Connell, & Cross, 2004).

Research on the use of MI for academic and behavioral improvement is also growing. For instance, two randomized controlled trials showed that even a single MI counseling session (50 minutes with a trained provider) for middle school students (typically ages 11 to 13) led to improvements in class participation, academic behavior, and higher math grades (Strait et al., 2012; Terry, Smith, Strait, & McQuillin, 2013). Another randomized trial found that two group sessions based on MI led to better math, science, and history grades than for students attending a single session of MI (Terry, Strait, McQuillin, & Smith, 2014). One pilot study has looked at truancy and found that a hybrid intervention of MI and other methods was successful among adolescents ages 16 and 17 (Enea & Dafinoiu, 2009). Encouraging research is also underway to explore how school consultants can use MI to aid teachers and parents to adopt effective strategies to help students improve their learning and behavior (Herman, Frey, Shephard, & Reinke, 2013).

We have supported MI training in at least 47 languages worldwide. The interest is there, and colleagues in countries like Estonia, Wales, and Poland are looking at adaptation in school to everyday teaching practice.

MI is complementary to whatever else you do to encourage change in students. In fact, most of the above applications are examples of MI *in combination with* one or more other interventions. This is consistent with how MI is often used in other settings and with other age groups.

Relationship

Promoting change has relationship at its heart, and motivation to change is the everyday challenge faced by all who wish to make things better for students. As the quotation that opened this chapter put it, "It really all depends on how the teachers and students interact." The next chapter provides a more detailed overview of MI, and acts as a map for the chapters to follow.

What Is MI?

People are better persuaded by the reasons
they have themselves discovered than by those
that come into the minds of others.
                                        —*Blaise Pascal*

There are lots of legitimate ways to improve motivation among students, and MI is one of them. MI flourishes through conversation that brings students alive, allowing you to notice improvements in their motivation by the look on their faces, the language they use, and the progress they make. This brief chapter provides an overview of MI, a map to guide you through the chapters to follow in the rest of Part I.

About Change

Struggles with motivation to change among students are widespread. MI has a focus on change and improving motivation, with a specific goal in mind, whether this is in attitude or behavior. The focus might be on academic performance, a potentially wide range of behavioral issues, or the student's well-being as a whole. Conversations about change are part of the normal, routine fabric of school life, occurring every day, and this book is about how to navigate them in a productive way. The first page of Chapter 1 highlighted some examples, and there are many more in Part II. Some are straightforward and require little thought, like asking a group of students to close their books and change their focus, while others, many others, are more complex, and might benefit from the use of MI.

The topic of change comes up like a signpost in all sorts of situations. Some of them are clear and obvious, while others emerge in the course of speaking with a student, perhaps about something else; then a signal emerges like a flag above a crowd, and you think to yourself, "We could talk about change now. . . . I can see the opportunity. . . . " That's when the guidelines in this book should be useful, to help you notice this, and to sharpen your ability to proceed efficiently and with a keen eye on a satisfying outcome.

Other Uses

While MI itself focuses on change conversations, other uses for the ideas and techniques in this book might soon become apparent. For example, one of the first tasks in learning about and practicing MI is to engage with a student, to use listening skills to connect with him or her, and to improve your relationship. While you might not end up talking about change and using MI itself, the efficient use of engaging can yield outcomes of all kinds. So too, if a student is angry, upset, confused, or disengaged, these skills help to calm things down and clarify how the student is feeling, whether or not you decide to focus on change.

> *The efficient use of engaging can yield outcomes of all kinds.*

Definitions

There are different ways of describing MI, some more technical than others. Here are five examples, starting with the broad and ending with the most technical.

- A conversation that helps someone work out why and how he or she might change.
- The opposite of direct persuasion: instead of trying to instill motivation from the outside, you encourage students to find it in themselves.
- A collaborative conversation style for strengthening a person's own motivation and commitment to change (Miller & Rollnick, 2013).

- A person-centered counseling style for addressing the common problem of ambivalence about change (Miller & Rollnick, 2013).
- A helping conversation in which you come alongside the student in the role of a guide, focus on the language he or she uses when talking about change, and then employ skills like reflective listening to reinforce this, thereby promoting change.

You'll notice that the challenge here is a bit like using words to describe a dance form. It's subtle, and involves both matters of style, what we have called the "spirit of MI" (see Chapter 3), and technical steps that are used to navigate the conversation, what we have called "core skills," described in Chapter 5. One can't exist without the other, and the essence of both is described below.

Foundations

Three foundations that MI rests on will likely be familiar because they correspond to foundations of good practice in schools and beyond. They are, first, guiding rather than leading; second, focusing on strengths and aspirations; and third, adopting an accepting and curious stance with students.

About Coming Alongside . . .

To highlight "coming alongside" as a foundation for learning and change is to risk stating the obvious in a school setting. Yet in everyday conversations, when it often feels like you are on an express train hurtling toward better performance, this principle can be overshadowed by talking down to students, talking at them, and trying to instill motivation into them.

MI is based not on standing in front of a student and pulling her toward change, or on standing behind her and pushing, but on coming alongside, and gently helping her to focus on change and see the way ahead. This familiar coming alongside is not based on sitting back passively, let alone allowing

MI is based not on standing in front of a student and pulling him or her toward change, or on standing behind him or her and pushing, but on coming alongside.

students forge their own paths, but on an active process of *guiding*, to be clarified in the next chapter.

A Person, with Dreams and Strengths

This foundation might be made most visible by asking a simple question, "What lens do you wear?," or put another way, "Do you look at a student as someone with weaknesses and problems or as someone with dreams and strengths?" (see Corbett, 2009). Consider these two accounts *of the same student:*

> "She is frankly disobedient, even rude sometimes, and her grades reflect someone who has failed to grasp the opportunities offered to her. Her peer relationships are troubled, and she. . . ."

> "Maria is working hard to get on top of life after her parents separated, and she misses her baby brother who does not live in her house any more. She makes sure she gets to school on time. However, when she's there, nothing seems to make sense, and she. . . ."

MI cannot flourish if someone like Maria is viewed only through the overwhelmingly negative lens of weakness and problems. It's like trying to grow a sunflower in a shady, infertile field. Focusing on strengths and aspirations does not mean ignoring problems or weaknesses, simply that they will become apparent to the student in the slipstream of a conversation charged with a more positive quality, and thus will be more likely to promote change. People change when they feel some freedom to choose and because they see that this will bring positive things for themselves, not just to avoid problems. Put another way, their own (intrinsic) motivation is a powerful force that you can harness in conversation.

In Conversations . . . Guided by Acceptance and Curiosity

MI draws its strength from the partnerships with and acceptance of students. Not necessarily acceptance of all behavior, it rather accepts each student as a person worthy of respect and able to steer his or her own life. From this accepting stance, your curiosity about the student naturally takes over as you explore his or her ideas about change, supported by your skills as a guide.

MI draws its strength from the partnerships with and acceptance of students.

What Is MI? 15

Upon these foundations for a conversation about change it's a relatively small step to using MI itself, in which you purposefully point the conversation toward change and encourage the student to say how and why it might happen. That's what we mean by evoking.

The Heart of MI: Evoking

MI involves a switch in mind-set when it comes to improving motivation, from persuading and cajoling, to drawing this motivation out from the student him- or herself. This defining characteristic of MI, which we call evoking, involves helping a student to come to a new understanding about change in the face of uncertainty or ambivalence, using his or her own words to resolve the challenge ahead. We have noticed this process of evoking unfolding naturally in the schools, where the restraint and patience of the teacher bear rich rewards. Our goal in this book is to translate what we have learned in MI so that you can sharpen your ability to recognize opportunities, and refine your skills to make better use of them. This is often a matter of noticing the "change language" that students use, and encouraging that language in a way that allows the students to express what they really want. Here's an example.

An Example with Signposts to Chapters in Part I

For the purposes of illustration and to embrace as much of MI as possible, the scenario below involves waving a magic wand over a teacher and student who manage the ideal—a series of brief conversations about change, with a good outcome. We appreciate that this is hard to reach in a typical busy day at school. Yet we also know from stories we hear that, bit by bit, conversation by conversation, students are touched by skillful educators, and remarkable change follows, sometimes slowly and discreetly, but significant nonetheless, not just in students, but in the fabric of school culture and all the relationships embraced by it.

Here's how our "ideal" conversation string unfolded over a period of weeks. The teacher approached a huddle of students in the playground, in heated disagreement about an Internet post that got nasty. Disciplinary action was not needed on this occasion. Kathy started telling the teacher her version of what had occurred; he avoided blame and punishment, and simply listened, summarizing for her what he had heard. She calmed down, and they agreed to talk after school. In the second conversation, which lasted 5–10 minutes, she again said how she was feeling about the fight and about how she was upset about a small group of peers goading her. The teacher invited her to look ahead and wondered aloud how she might get through these situations more comfortably, with less threat of conflict and consequences. Kathy looked at him with wide eyes, not expecting the question. The teacher heard her say she how she would like to be different, and spent a few minutes exploring exactly what that might mean, giving space to Kathy describe it herself. The incident wasn't resolved, and the teacher encouraged her to think about the question, knowing they would speak again soon. The next day he approached her, and she had thought about it. He affirmed her courage, tracked very carefully what she said about change, and focused on it; he summarized it for her when he heard it, and she seemed to break through into clarity. She resolved to try to do something differently: "I'm going to take five every time they have a go at me. I'm not going to let them get to me, even if I have to turn away and walk off. . . . I'll let you know if it keeps happening." The outcome was favorable: Kathy put this new idea into practice, let the teacher know in a brief catch-up conversation, and felt more in control of how she handled situations like this.

That's an ordinary conversation about a common occurrence and MI was at its center. The key elements are highlighted below, along with reference to the chapters to follow that go into the topic in more detail.

The Style and the Spirit of MI

In Chapter 3 we summarize the underlying guiding style and mindset involved when using MI. For this teacher, restraint was a starting point. He avoided using the righting reflex to solve the problem for Kathy and instead came alongside her with a compassionate, accepting, and curious attitude, assuming that Kathy had much of the wisdom inside her about how she might solve the problem. It was his job to provide a comfortable scaffold for the conversation, with a focus on her ideas about change. The evoking process described above came to life as Kathy formed a plan that made sense to her.

Four Processes

In Chapter 4 we provide a map for the conversation about change in the form of four steps, evident in the above exchanges. The teacher *engaged* first before doing anything else, then purposefully provided a *focus* or direction for their conversations: that is, to make better headway with peers and avoid upset. Then he moved on to a third step, *evoking*, when he encouraged her to say how and why she might change. Finally, they moved into the *planning* process where he supported her to come up with her own solutions.

Core Skills

In Chapter 5 we review and illustrate the core conversation skills that are a foundation for MI and that can be more broadly useful in education as a whole. These core skills are the tools you use to navigate an MI conversation. These were artfully used by the teacher to address the problem efficiently in a conversation that had Kathy's needs and strengths at its center. *Open questions* were used to start conversations about how she felt and, critically, about how she saw the way ahead. *Reflective listening*, or brief summaries of what she had said, was used to encourage her to amplify and clarify her thinking, especially when the topic was positive change in the future. Accurate reflections create and strengthen engagement and tell the student he or she has been heard and understood. They create momentum for change. *Affirmations*, verbal acknowledgments of her strengths, gave the teacher an opportunity to help Kathy see these for herself. *Summaries* were used to bring segments of conversation to a close, to highlight the positives, and to make way for a new topic or direction for the conversation.

> *MI's core skills are the tools you use to navigate a conversation.*

Evoking Change Talk

In Chapter 6 we explore and illustrate the very heart of MI, evoking the student's own motivation to change. In the above example the teacher used the core skills to purposefully elicit what we call *change talk*, the language Kathy used as she found her own reasons to change. He evoked this with a single thoughtful question when he "invited her to look ahead and wondered aloud how she might get through these situations more comfortably." The answers, mixed with other things, included change talk. Chapter 6 provides guidelines for responding to change talk to get the best out of students.

Planning Changes

In Chapter 7 we illustrate how the same style and core skills can be used when constructing a change plan with students. On this occasion with

Kathy, in line with an idealized scenario, it was simple: the teacher elicited a concrete plan from Kathy quite quickly when he summarized her unfolding ideas and positive motivations, and asked her something like, "I wonder what you might do in the future." The plan emerged, she committed to it, and they enjoyed her account of success in a brief follow-up conversation. It's often not always so simple, and the need to remain alongside and avoid the righting reflex might be paramount as you work on change plans with students. Advice is often called for.

Giving Advice and Information

In Chapter 8 we broaden the focus considerably to address the very common challenge of giving information and advice to students. In the above scenario Kathy did not seem to need or want this, but there are many who do. How might the style and skills of MI improve the conduct and outcome of giving information and advice? We provide some practical guidelines in Chapter 8.

The Routes Ahead

In this chapter we used the scenario with Kathy not only to highlight the main features of MI, but also to convey the idea that while MI can be used in a prearranged conversation, its benefit can be realized in the spontaneous everyday conversations you have with students.

MI is compatible with good teaching practice and complements the skills you already use. You choose a moment—and there are scores of these every day—to focus on change, and you use MI to help students find a way forward, and express their own good reasons to you. It is useful in both quiet conversations about change and for taking the heat out of conflict. In Part II, where we work through examples of everyday application, you'll notice many that involve quite difficult situations where a student is very angry or upset. How to calm things down quickly and constructively is a challenge well suited to MI.

The chapters in Part I to follow go into each of the topics covered above. The examples in Part II further bring to life the core skills, four processes, and spirit of MI as applied in common school situations. Part III illustrates more focused applications. In Part IV we broaden the perspective. Uniting all of these chapters is our view that relationships, empathy, and constructive conversations sit at the center of learning and change.

MI is like walking down a path with a student, wide enough to be alongside each other, while you take care not to veer off into thorny undergrowth. One teacher came out of an MI-informed conversation with a student and proclaimed, "It's like 'staying in the groove,' and I never realized how it was possible to steer a conversation in this way." Our hope is that the chapters to follow equip you with the wherewithal to do just this.

The Spirit and Style of MI

Children have never been very good at
listening to their elders, but they have never
failed to imitate them.
—*James Baldwin*

In this chapter we describe the spirit and style of MI, or put another way, the mind-set and "heart-set" that lies behind the spoken word. A guiding style, described below, provides a solid foundation for understanding and using MI.

Three Communication Styles

Box 3.1 describes three communication styles commonly used to tackle different problems. Many situations call for the communication style of directing. A student asks for or clearly needs help, and you explain and advise accordingly. Here you are the expert, and the student follows your lead. At the other end of the spectrum is the style of following, perhaps used less often. For example, a student bursts into tears on arrival at school; something has happened, and you know that your best approach is to simply listen, and allow her to tell you her story.

Between these approaches is a style that in many ways takes the best of both: guiding. You listen but you also provide information, and

---

BOX 3.1. Three Communication Styles

Directing	Guiding	Following
Teaching	Drawing out	Listening
Instructing	Encouraging	Understanding
Leading	Motivating	Going along with

---

your attitude is one of helping students find the way ahead, rather than solving the problem for them. Close to the heart of skillful teaching, this style is particularly suited to helping students change their behavior and acquire new skills. It serves as the foundation for MI.

Guiding is often forsaken in favor of a directing style. Why this happens is an interesting question. One possibility is that in the often-pressurized world of action, with everyone scurrying here and there addressing this and that challenge, it seems easier to instill motivation by simply telling students why and how they should change.

The Guiding Style: The Foundation of MI

It was in a counseling setting in the early 1980s that William R. Miller uncovered the enormous potential of a guiding style when faced with apparently intractable problems of low motivation among people entrenched in denial about their behavioral problems. Tempting as it might have been to direct and use the righting reflex (see Chapter 1), he found that

> when I sat back, avoided trying to solve the problem for the person, and came alongside them with a helpful attitude, I found I could gently steer them to face the future and say for themselves how things might be different. Their motivation to change improved in front of my eyes. (William R. Miller, personal communication)

The simplicity of this account probably belies the skillfulness with which Miller navigated some very tough conversations. Over the following 30 years we refined the techniques described in this book, and overcame some familiar challenges, like how to speak with "difficult" or angry people, or those feeling prickly, sensitive, or ambivalent about change.

Consider the difference between these two interventions:

"You just need to concentrate harder to get this job done."
"What's going to really help you to get the job done?"

These offerings are quite different starting points for motivating students to change. The first effort, delivered in a directing style, seems based on a conviction that learning is impeded by something the student *lacks,* in this case, concentration, and that it's the teacher's job to insert this wisdom into the mind of the student. Deficit is the focus. The statement might well be true in some way, but is it effective? Resistance from the student is a strong possibility. The second sentence uses a guiding style and asks the student to work out what the answer is. It can be a much more effective platform for learning.

While each style has its place, choosing which one to use when can be a challenge. One broad guideline came from a colleague who was learning MI: "I'm shifting a little more into the center in how I handle people [see Box 3.1]. I try to stand with two feet planted firmly in the guiding style, and shift to either side as necessary." With MI, the center ground is a good place to start when you face the need to talk about change in behavior or attitude.

Guiding cannot happen without a goal in mind. For example, a parent guides a child who is completing a puzzle. They are engaged and absorbed, almost like in a dance. Ideas will pass to and fro, *with the child leading the way.* The parent makes a suggestion here and there ("Maybe look at this piece . . . ") and uses questions that have a searching and purposeful quality designed for the child to answer ("Might this work?" or "Where do you think this piece goes?"). *The essence of guiding is an attitude that assumes the child can find the answer.* Engagement is critical. Autonomy is reinforced naturally, with understated words and phrases that maximize freedom of choice for the child ("*Maybe* look at this piece" or "*Might* this work?").

> *Guiding cannot happen without a goal in mind.*

Transfer this example into a school setting and it starts to look a lot like effective teaching, observable also in a skilled sports coach. The style is simple to use, requires restraint and patience, and it can be threatened by circumstance. Both parties need to feel comfortable and not distracted. Distraction can take many forms for teachers, for example, feeling tired or irritated. What happens next under these circumstances is most likely you will either withdraw, following the learner and not providing enough structure, or you will provide too much structure using a directing style ("No, don't put the piece there, put it here"). Either way the optimal conditions for learning will be impaired and a disinterested or distracted learner is a likely outcome.

At the heart of guiding is helping a learner to self-regulate. Detachment doesn't help much, and overinvolvement can be crippling and undermine learning. Guiding sits in the middle ground between these two. The conversation skills for doing this effectively are the focus for all to follow in this book. "Scaffolding" is a phrase often used to describe this process, and "Socratic questioning" has been presented as a way of promoting it. Here are some examples of questions informed by a guiding style:

> "What ideas do you have that will help you with getting to school on time?"
> "How do you see yourself making it through these next few weeks while still maintaining your goal of passing your exams?"
> "[to a whole class] What are some ideas that you all have for the best ways to study for next week's exam?"
> "What sorts of things have you done in the past that have helped you avoid getting in fights?"
> "How do you imagine staying in class even though you don't see eye to eye with your teacher?"
> "What are some of the benefits of graduating for you?"

The above questions can be misunderstood, just as MI can be misunderstood. A disregard for the spirit of MI is the most common problem we encounter. Without it, the approach can be seen as an expert way of getting students to do something they would not otherwise want to do, like a trick or technique for effecting the required behavior change. We once heard this caricature of MI: "Getting someone to do what you want them to do but making them think it's their idea." This way of viewing a change conversation is really just a variant of the righting reflex, seeing a problem and using this or that method to fix it for students. The conversation will unfortunately soon become troubled. The student will notice it and frustration for both parties will surface quite soon.

The Spirit of MI

We developed the phrase "the spirit of MI" to convey what it means to be an effective guide, so that when a student is talking about change, this "spirit" or mind-set serves as a reminder about what's involved.

The spirit of MI is captured by four words: "compassion," "partnership," "acceptance," and "evocation." The spirit of MI lives and breathes with an attitude like this: "I'd like to help you [compassion] and talk this through with you [partnership]; you are a valuable person and I will refrain from judging you [acceptance]; instead, I'd like to listen and find out what you think will work well for you to change [evocation]." There are two strands here: one describes the relationship with your students (compassion, partnership, acceptance), the other is curiosity about the language students use as you help them talk about change (evocation), whether the goal is solving a math puzzle or solving persistent lateness for class. We'll cover each of these strands in turn below.

The three elements of compassion, partnership and acceptance are readily observable below in the first statement to a student, and missing in the second statement.

> "You are trying hard, this isn't easy, and you are hoping this chat we are having might help a bit."
> "I can tell you that you're not trying hard enough, and that's why we are having this chat."

Words reflect your attitude. The first statement is encouraging and helpful while the second is based on fear and intimidation as motivators of change. If you want to help a student to change, your attitude of partnership with, acceptance of, and compassion for your student will make all the difference. This is borne out not only in theory and research on learning, but in the stories of students themselves. Ask anyone who their favorite schoolteacher was and why, and these relational elements come shining through: "She believed in me, so I started focusing in school more and learned a lot." Let's take a closer look at the qualities of compassion, partnership, and acceptance.

Compassion

This word is often equated with feelings of warmth and caring for another person. While people who work with youth often feel this way, the use of compassion in MI involves an active commitment to meet a student's needs, guided largely by the student's goals and values.

> *Compassion in MI involves an active commitment to meet a student's needs.*

Partnership

A partnership is a collaboration between experts. You, an expert on the subject matter and teaching methods, are working with students who are experts on themselves. As with any relationship, such partnerships can be slow to develop, and require attention to build trust. With some students, this will be fairly straightforward, with others it will require more persistence.

Acceptance

If students sense acceptance as human beings, from someone willing to seek out their strengths and be respectful of their needs, they will be more likely to change. A key element of acceptance is support for student autonomy. We all know what acceptance feels like on the receiving end. It's sometimes hard to practice acceptance with students in a busy school environment. It's worth noting that you do not have to agree with a student's behavior to accept him or her as a young person worthy of attention with the potential to change; neither is acceptance the same as acquiescence, as going along with whatever the student says or wants. It is, however, refraining from being judgmental.

Acceptance of student autonomy is not just a state of mind. It can be expressed in the way you ask questions, in your body language, in the way you use core skills (Chapter 5), and in the nuances of word choice. You can find some examples in this book's Part II. Partnership, compassion, and acceptance can be sensed whenever people try to help others learn and change. The fourth word capturing the spirit of MI is evocation, which can be seen in the practice of a skillful guide.

Evocation

Evocation means to actively draw out from students their perspectives about change. It's the opposite of telling students why or how they should change. Curiosity is crucial here for engaging with an open mind, and searching for how a student might develop a new approach to change. Then you will notice something: students use language that expresses their aspirations about change, however mild this might be. It's the key to success, and we have called it "change talk." Change talk can look like this:

"I could try to stay after for extra help."
"One thing I will do is turn off my phone at night."

"I don't like fighting with him."
"If I fail this class, I'm off the team."

These statements, and the countless others like them, are expressions of a student's desire for and belief in their ability to change.

Approaching students with partnership, compassion, acceptance, and curiosity sounds a lot like what good teachers do naturally, and it is. MI provides you with the conversational techniques to do this even better, including how to do it in tough situations where someone's motivation appears to be low. The next chapter provides a map of change conversations to help you navigate them as smoothly as possible.

> *Evocation is the opposite of telling students why or how they should change.*

A Conversation Map

Four Processes

> When we are no longer able to change
> a situation, we are challenged to change
> ourselves.
> —*Viktor Frankl*

We have identified four conversational patterns that facilitate change: engaging, focusing, evoking, and planning. These four processes provide a map of routes through change conversations. The processes build on one another, and moving through them is like walking up four steps, to be illustrated in this chapter. The initial steps need to be in good shape; you might need to step back down at any point. One word of caution: it's unwise to think of these processes as things you do to a student. They refer to what happens between you and the student, in the relationship, which is why we refer to them as processes.

Engaging: The First Step

Engaging is a process of actively establishing a connection and a helpful working relationship with the student. It does not mean simply talking with a student in a friendly way. It is much more than that

27

and involves reaching out to show the student that you understand his or her experience and aspirations, untainted by your own views and interjections. The collaborative spirit of MI is crucial for engaging, and the technical core skills for doing this are described in the next chapter.

You'll notice when engagement is not there, when two people talk about change *without* a sense of being on a helpful journey together. Get engaging right, and the journey and its outcome will be a whole lot easier. Sometimes engagement can occur within minutes, other times it takes much longer.

How many children pass through lessons, classes, and hallways for years without feeling interpersonally engaged by any school staff member? It's a harrowing question. Then when problems arise, the absence of engagement can stand out like a burned finger, and those involved can fall into a cycle of labeling and blaming on the one side, and denial, defending, and acting out on the other. The same patterns existed in the tough world of addiction treatment where MI was born. The lesson learned there was that a judgmental attitude can be part of a vicious cycle—the negative attitude of others further undermines engagement and performance. We discovered that a shift in our style, toward strong interpersonal engagement, helped to break the cycle (see Figure 4.1).

Engagement does not involve a lengthy counseling session. This book contains many examples of what we have called "rapid engagement," where the skillful use of listening to engage a student reaps immediate rewards. Skillful practice saves time. Engaging is the first step in MI but it needs to continue throughout the conversation. Keep

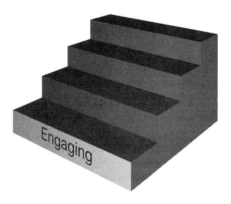

FIGURE 4.1. Engaging: Establish a helping relationship.

engagement alive at all times, and the other processes can be of help. Another lesson is this: when there's trouble, confusion, upset, or anger, engage before all else.

Engaging, on its own, might not be enough. It can become part of a cozy relationship that fails to make progress. Sympathy for the student, which is different from *Engagement is the first step, but it needs to continue throughout the conversation.*

empathy, can fuel what we might call a "pastoral reflex,"[1] in which the two parties wrap themselves in a cocoon that is hard for the student to break out of. That's where the second process can be useful—it helps to focus the conversation on change, to get things moving in a positive direction.

Focusing: The Second Step

Focusing is an observable process that describes how people in a conversation decide what change to talk about, and which direction the conversation should go in (see Figure 4.2). Sometimes this is unnecessary and obvious to both parties, and as they engage, the horizon or purpose of the conversation is clear, and off they go, as with many change conversations in school. For example, there is a question about math results, and improvement is a natural focus.

Then there are situations where the horizon is not so clear, where

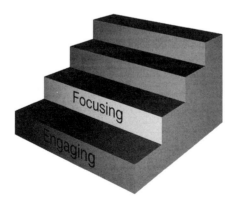

FIGURE 4.2. Focusing: Agree on a useful direction.

[1]Thanks to Dr. Andy Williams for suggesting this term.

you engage with a student, and a number of discrete possibilities for focusing the conversation open up, and there is a need to funnel the conversation in a useful direction. How to do this is illustrated in many places in Part II.

Focusing is funneling the conversation in a useful direction.

Evoking: The Third Step

Evoking is the process of drawing out the student's ideas about why and how to change (see Figure 4.3). It is the heart of MI and requires the earlier two processes—engaging and focusing—to be alive and clear. It has been highlighted a number of times in earlier chapters, and stands out as one that is particularly strong in our accounts of MI, refined over many years, an observable pattern that seems to lift motivation to change: the student, rather than you, talks about why and how he or she might change, guided by your curiosity and attention to the language of change.

Evoking involves pointing the conversation toward change, guided by your attention to the student's "change talk." You encourage change talk by reflecting it (a core skill) and asking open questions (another core skill) like, "How might you get through these difficult situations more comfortably?"

How you spot and stay with a student's change talk to evoke change is the subject of Chapter 6; many examples from everyday school life

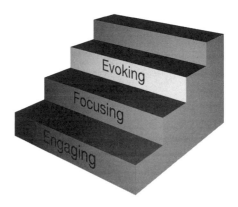

FIGURE 4.3. Evoking: Draw out ideas about change.

are provided in Part II. A point comes, however, when determination to change meets a new challenge, actually putting it into practice. That's the next process.

Planning: The Fourth Step

Planning is the process of helping the student decide how to make the change, what to do, and when (see Figure 4.4), and in MI, it sits on the foundation of the other three processes. Indeed, planning and evoking merge readily when you draw out of students what a good plan might look and feel like. Planning is so familiar that it can be hard to notice, like a permanently blue sky. So why bother to discuss it? A student wants to do something, " . . . so go ahead and do it," surely?

Planning is so familiar that it can be hard to notice.

One answer is that the changes are often not simple for a student, and require effort, courage, foresight, and thoughtfulness in the face of failure. Ambivalence or uncertainty doesn't go away just because someone makes an initial decision to change.

If you as the teacher enter this scenario with a "just do it" approach, fueled by the righting reflex and many good intentions, you are likely to meet resistance from the student, as we described in the opening of Chapter 1.

Students need, and often want, information and advice. Engagement

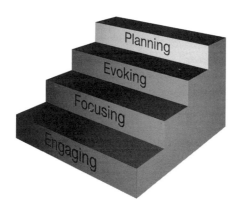

FIGURE 4.4. Planning: If ready, explore action.

is like glue that binds you while you clarify aspirations, search for solutions, and examine choices with them. How to use MI spirit and skills to do this is described in Chapters 7 and 8.

These four steps can be presented in a sequence that carries a risk of oversimplification, the most common being the idea that when you have done with one step, you don't need to worry about it again. Their usefulness will come to life in the illustrated examples in Part II, where one of the strongest implications should become apparent: be careful of jumping up the steps too quickly, or missing a step or two. Their smooth functioning requires skill, and this is the subject of the next chapter.

Core Skills

If the only tool you have is a hammer, you
tend to see every problem as a nail.
—*Abraham Maslow*

In this chapter we pay attention to only a few of the many ingredients
of effective communication. Four core skills are highlighted: (ask)
Open questions, Affirm, Reflect, and Summarize (OARS). We focus
first on what these skills are and how they are used in MI to enhance
engagement. We then discuss how the skills can be combined effectively. Skillful conversations are efficient; they get to the heart of things
quickly without losing the essential engagement that is the foundation
for success.

To see a good demonstration of the usefulness of the core skills,
watch a skillful television interviewer in a talk show. You'll see the
skills in action and may be surprised at how often reflection is used to
save time and maximize progress. Under considerable pressure, a skillful talk show host can manage to keep focus and use these skills with
ease, including the use of pauses to finesse the conversation. It takes
practice to perfect their use.

The Role of Empathy

These skills are used throughout MI conversations to create and maintain empathy with students. Empathy is different from sympathy. It

does not mean feeling sorry for a student. Instead, empathy enables engagement and occurs when you and the student create a connection of shared understanding of the student's experience. It's not hard to spot when you feel you are really understanding the student and you notice that the student does too. One of the main aims of this chapter is to illustrate how this connection can be established skillfully and efficiently to improve not just engagement, but to establish a focus and create a platform for evoking change, the subject of the next chapter.

Listening with skill is at the heart of creating empathy. More than concentrating or imagining the student's experience, listening is a very active process during which you "reflect back" to students what you have heard them say or try to say. This helps you connect with them in a powerful way. Listening and reflect-

Listening with skill is at the heart of creating empathy.

ing are useful in a wide range of circumstances, from calming down the angry student to prompting him or her to face change.

The Pace of a Conversation

The pacing of a conversation matters. The space between words is often as important as the words themselves. A rat-a-tat-tat, quick-paced conversation might be helpful and essential in some situations, but not all the time, and certainly not if motivating change in students is the focus. If the pace is slowed down a little, progress can be faster, because the student has time to absorb, reflect, and move forward, and you have time to offer a helpfully worded question or reflection. A pause of half a second can feel much longer and fill the exchange with added gravitas and meaning. It's a paradoxical phenomenon noticed by many observers of human interaction, indeed, even with training of horses: Monty Roberts, the original "horse whisperer," apparently commented, "Act like I've got all day, and it will take 15 minutes. Act like I've only got 15 minutes, and it will take all day."

Open Questions (The "O" in "OARS")

Asking open questions will open up the conversation, and in MI one relies much more on open than closed questions. Closed questions invite a restricted range of answers, such as "yes" or "no." They can be useful for nailing down a fact or two in your conversation, or for pointing to a very significant issue; for example, "Are you OK?"; "Would you like to come to my office?"; or "Are you feeling upset about this?" Using *only* closed questions makes for a very stilted conversation and the person would soon wonder whether you are playing some kind of guessing game.

Open questions invite a wide range of possible answers, not just "yes" or "no." "How," "What," and "Why" are excellent first words for an open question; for example, "Why did this happen?"; "What happened then?" Another simple question is to ask something like "Tell me more about how you are feeling."

One feature of questions, whether open or closed, is that the energy and direction for the unfolding conversation comes from the asker. An open key question can be critical for steering the conversation in a productive direction. However, if all you do is ask questions, the student can become passive and disempowered, exactly the opposite of what you want to achieve with MI.

> *If all you do is ask questions, the student can become passive.*

Consider the pattern in the dialogue below, which has a decidedly lopsided quality. A student, Kathy, used as an example in Chapter 2, approaches a teacher about a small group of peers. She looks upset.

TEACHER: What happened? [Open question]

KATHY: Out there in the playground, there was a group of us, and she showed me this posting and laughed at me.

TEACHER: What's her name? [Closed question]

KATHY: (*Gives the name.*)

TEACHER: Did she hurt you? [Closed question]

KATHY: No, she posted this horrible picture of me.

TEACHER: When did she do that? [Closed question]

KATHY: Just now, this morning.

TEACHER: And how did you react? [Open question]

This very common pattern leaves the interviewer firmly in charge of coming up with the next question, with a relatively passive recipient. Imagine a talk show interview conducted along these lines. The conversation will not flow very well, because it is likely to fall back in a stilted way on whatever is the next question. For the receiver, the experience will be of the conversation changing direction in unpredictable ways and of being on the receiving end of something approaching an investigation.

One useful feature of open questions is the opportunity they provide to focus on change in the student, a bit like using the rudder to shift the direction of a boat. They provide a forward-looking momentum. Put another way, they are used in the service of a guiding style (see Chapter 3) because a guide is usually focused on where you want to go. For example, "What would you most like to talk about?" (i.e., what's the focus?) or "How might you handle this next time?" (i.e., evoking solution from the student).

After asking an open question, it's the student's turn to explore the answer. Of course, the student may not respond fully, most commonly because she might be confused or not feel yet that you are genuinely interested in her answers. That's where the next two skills, affirming and reflection, help a lot.

Affirm (The "A" in "OARS")

Imagine the teacher saying to that student Kathy, "That would have taken some courage." That's an affirmation; its essence is the teacher pointing to the student's strengths, efforts, achievements, and good qualities during a conversation. It's not delivered as a judgment, like praise ("Well done, Kathy, you showed lots of courage there"); this might be helpful, but it is not quite the same thing. Other examples are:

"You are someone who wants friends who are loyal, because that's what you are."
"Even when you are upset you make careful decisions."

Affirming is less of a judgment and more like shining a light on something positive inside the student. You notice this; you tell the student, who notices it too, and the effect of this apparently small gesture often matters more than it is given credit for. The look on the student's face will reveal the impact. Kathy was no doubt feeling overwhelmed by threats and negative images of herself when she approached the teacher. An affirmation can cut through this and feed her with courage to move on, no doubt where the word "encourage" comes from.

Affirming is like shining a light on something positive in the student.

The famous educator Sir Ken Robinson (2014), revisiting his old school in a poor district of Liverpool, England, reflected, "When you're that young, it doesn't take a lot to be encouraged, or discouraged . . . they raised my game . . . they saw something in me I didn't see in myself." Affirmation probably played its part.

Behind an affirmation lies an open-minded willingness to notice positive things about a student. This is sometimes hard when faced with a student who seems to have a list of problems written on his forehead. It's one thing to help a student see what went wrong, quite another to "raise his game" with an affirmation.

Reflect (The "R" in "OARS")

To reflect is to repeat in different words what you have heard the student say or perhaps what he or she was trying to say. As with questions, reflections can be used within any of the four processes described in Chapter 4: to come alongside a student and connect (engaging); to establish the direction of a conversation (focusing); to give the student space to consider change (evoking); and to put decisions into practice (planning). A conversation might typically start with an open question, followed by a few reflections before the next open question changes the direction a little. Reflections are the lifeblood of skillful practice. Kathy's teacher wants her to be active, engaged, and talking freely about her challenge and so he used a number of reflections.

> TEACHER: (*after hearing her story for a while*) And how did you react? [Open question]
>
> KATHY: I dunno, I just lost it.
>
> TEACHER: You were that upset. [Reflection]
>
> KATHY: Yeah, I was, and she ran off laughing with her group of loser friends.
>
> TEACHER: And that must have left you feeling more upset. [Reflection, a guess about what she must have felt]
>
> KATHY: No, I was angry then. I wanted to take her head off, then I had no one to turn to.
>
> TEACHER: So what did you do? [Open question]
>
> KATHY: Well, you saw me and so I told you.
>
> TEACHER: That would have taken some courage. [Affirmation]
>
> KATHY: (*Looks up.*) She can't do that again and I don't want her as a friend.

TEACHER: You don't like girls who do that to you. [Reflection]

KATHY: No, that's right, she's a bitch—I can tell you that for sure. There was no reason to do that. I had done nothing to upset her. She just wants to be the queen bee around here and makes it hard for others and I don't want a friend like that.

TEACHER: So you are now wondering about what friends you don't want and what friends you do want. [Reflection]

KATHY: Yeah, for sure that's a good question, I am learning what I don't want.

TEACHER: And that helps. [Reflection]

KATHY: It does, so maybe I need to find other friends.

TEACHER: What might that involve? [Open question]

The above brief illustration offers a map of how to use reflection, affirmation, and open questions. Reflections are used to engage with Kathy, calm her down, and help her consider change and improvement. The teacher used his natural curiosity to ask three open questions and then made an affirmation followed by statements reflecting the essence of what Kathy said. As shown in the example, reflections can also be derived from nonverbal cues, and guesses about what a student means or is feeling. These served as an invitation to elaborate further, and Kathy was no longer passive, and probably felt in charge of what she said. A colleague from Norway was struggling to find a translation for "reflection" and eventually announced that maybe the best solution was to simply call it a "short summary" of what the person is saying. The teacher might well have said, "Yes, that's what I was doing."

Reflections usually begin with words and phrases like "You . . . "; "You feel . . . "; "It's . . . "; "It's like . . . "; "And you. . . . " Getting the first words of a reflection simple can be a steep learning curve for people practicing this talent for the first time. We often hear learners begin a reflection with, "What I'm hearing you say is. . . . " This can be a good way to get into the right frame of mind for making a reflection. With practice, learners soon drop this kind of preamble (the word "I" is not really necessary), and simply make the statement that flows from the preamble, for example, "You just don't like being treated like that." It can feel a bit scary at first just making a statement because control is being relinquished to the student. The rewards become apparent when the student continues the conversation with enhanced engagement and you both feel enhanced empathy.

Listening Is Not Passive, and Empathizing Is an Active Process

Listening gets a bad name in some quarters because it is misunderstood as simply sitting back passively and *hearing* a student's story. This not only takes a lot of time but can leave the two parties going around in circles. The form of listening described here involves hearing and understanding as a first step. The second step is then to actively convey this to the student. It's that second step, *offering a reflection,* that cements the connection, creates empathy, and, in MI, helps develop momentum toward change.

> *Offering a reflection cements the connection, creates empathy, and helps develop momentum toward change.*

Curiosity Promotes Change

Change conversations are best fueled by curiosity. Reflections are often guesses about what a student is meaning or feeling, and they demonstrate that you are listening and trying to understand. They give the student a chance to continue the story, and as you emit these reflections, the person comes to realize that you *must* understand them because otherwise you would not have said what you did. That in itself creates empathy. Then things can, and often do, change.

Listening and Reflecting Save Time

In the dialogue above, when Kathy said, "I just lost it," the teacher responded, "You were that upset." Kathy never said that, but the teacher used the reflection almost to finish her sentence for her. That saved Kathy from having to describe how upset she was because she felt that the teacher understood this. It's in this sense that listening can be efficient and save time.

Getting It Wrong: A Problem?

What if you offer a reflection and get it wrong? It happened in the above dialogue; Kathy simply corrected the teacher. This has been our experience. As long as the student feels that you are sincere in your intentions, it does not matter. Indeed it's a good sign when you are corrected because the student is actively trying to help you understand things. It's like a built-in coaching mechanism for improving your skillfulness.

Curiosity and a sense of direction from you are most of what's needed; being absolutely right is not the most important thing because you are taking an educated guess, the aim of which is to encourage the student to reflect, refine, and move forward.

Different Kinds of Reflection

In the conversation with Kathy, the teacher used different kinds of reflection. A *simple reflection* is the safest and often most useful of all—you just restate in different words what the student has said. A *complex reflection* adds new meaning and can be used to point the conversation in the direction of change, for example, "So you are now wondering about what friends you don't want and what friends you do want." A *double-sided reflection,* not used above, captures both sides of a student's dilemma; for example, the teacher might have said, "You like some of the girls but not one of them who was unkind to you." In the next chapter we will point to how these can be used to evoke change talk.

Multiple Uses, Same Outcome: A Better Relationship

A student is really angry, another is upset, and yet another is really confused. In each case reflection is a very effective and efficient way of opening up a calmer route, and for improving your relationship. You can do no harm in using it, and the more you practice, the easier it will become.

Summarize (The "S" in "OARS)

To summarize well means, first, listening and noticing the student's key points during the conversation, in readiness for producing them in a summary. This is how the teacher summarized things for Kathy:

> TEACHER: Kathy, I want to summarize what's been said so you can make sure I understand you, and then we'll think about where to go next, OK? You saw me and took a chance, which took courage. You told me the story, how you are feeling, and how you would like to find friends that don't behave like that. Have I missed anything?

KATHY: Yeah, that's me.

TEACHER: Can I suggest that. . . .

A summary brings together what's been said. It can take the form of a collection of short summaries. When Kathy said "Yeah, that's me," she confirmed that the teacher had listened and understood correctly. It also affirmed and solidified the progress she was making.

A summary also allows you to change direction, prompting one of our colleagues, a very busy administrator, to proclaim, "I get it. If I feel lost or it's going on too long, I just summarize and then we can move on."

You'll notice a couple of other features of the teacher's summary: he didn't use the word "I," but "you," because it's a summary of her concerns and aspirations. He was focused on her strengths, not just her problems, and he included an affirmation ("You saw me and took a chance, which took courage"). He made sure to invite Kathy to add anything he might have missed. Finally, a summary can be used to highlight what the student has said positively about change. We will say more about that issue in the next chapter on evoking.

> *A summary can highlight what the student has said positively about change.*

Combining Core Skills in Conversation

If a conversation about change is like music, the core skills are the notes you play. An open question that points to change is often followed by a reflection or two, or even more. Affirmation appears, then another open question, and the cycle is repeated until a summary brings things together.

Using the following abbreviations it becomes possible to see these patterns more clearly: Open questions (O); Reflections (r); Affirmations (a); Summary (S). An MI conversation will look something like this, repeated in cyclical fashion, with variations of course: O, r, r, r, a, O, r, r, O, r, r, r, a, S.

Box 5.1 summarizes the core skills with examples.

And MI?

Motivation to change, the subject of MI, has hardly been mentioned in this chapter, yet through the use of these core skills it has reared its

---

BOX 5.1. Examples of Core Skills

- **Open questions:** Inviting a wide range of possible answers.
  "What happened?"
  "How . . . ?"
  "Why . . . ?"
  "Tell me more. . . . "

- **Affirm:** Shining a light on student strengths and achievements.
  "That would have taken some courage."
  "You are determined to change things."
  "You worked really hard on that assignment."
  "When you are focused, you get things done."
  "You have the insight to realize what is going on."

- **Reflect:** Telling the student, in different words, what you heard the student say or mean.

  - *Simple reflection:*
    "You don't like girls that do that to you."
    "You're not able to get here on time."

  - *Complex reflection (in response to student saying, "I don't like being here at school like this"):*
    "You want things to change."

  - *Double-sided reflection:*
    "It's hard to enjoy this subject, yet you want to pass the class."
    "You don't want to hang out with those girls and yet you don't want to be alone on the playground."

- **Summarize:** Noting the student's key points during the conversation, and then producing the points in a summary. Use "you," include aspirations and strengths along with concerns. Ask the student if you missed anything.

---

head a number of times, well worth identifying by way of conclusion, if only to clarify that it is not something incredibly difficult from or different to a normal conversation with Kathy.

A first task in learning to use the skills in MI is to notice when the conversation is steered or veers toward change. Kathy's teacher was aware of this. When Kathy said things like "I don't want her as a friend" and "I don't want a friend like that," it was an expression of what she wants, a pointer to the goal of finding new friends, what we call change talk, and on both occasions the teacher didn't change the subject, but merely offered a reflection in reply. Then when it was time to summarize, the teacher once again highlighted these aspirations. The effect of this on her motivation to change was likely to be more positive than negative.

One word for this process of responding skillfully as a student builds her capacity to envision and realize change is "evoking," and that is MI, the subject of the next chapter, where the core skills are illustrated in the service of a guiding style.

Evoking

The Heart of MI

A moment's insight is sometimes worth a life's experience.

—*Oliver Wendell Holmes*

When educators use a guiding style to draw out their students' curiosity and problem-solving abilities, they are laying the foundations for evoking. This requires patience, and a belief that the person in front of you has the potential to learn and change. MI takes this process one step further. Your curiosity is focused on the language of change used by the student. Such change talk is a signpost of the student's motivation to change and you purposefully point the conversation in this direction with the spirit and skills described in earlier chapters. The heart of MI is noticing change talk and helping it to grow and solidify.

This chapter describes how to elicit change talk, notice it, and respond efficiently and effectively to it, thereby helping a student to come to a new understanding of a change in his or her life. It revolves around a single conversation for illustration purposes. We

Evoking requires a belief that the person in front of you has the potential to learn and change.

are mindful, however, that this is just a snapshot, and that multiple conversations over time, even brief ones, provide the fuel for growth and change in students.

Joe's Story: From Trouble to Useful Talk: Engaging and Focusing

Joe had seen more altercations and detentions than he could probably recall. For him, school was largely about getting into trouble and receiving low grades. Now he'd had his last warning before expulsion. A senior teacher with responsibility for his students' well-being called him aside.

The teacher's initial approach was an accepting one, with an invitation to "come and have a chat about your situation" after class. He told Joe that this would not be about discipline, but about him, and how he is feeling about school. That's probably why Joe turned up feeling not too defensive.

Knowing how often conversations about change fall at the first hurdle of engagement, the teacher "put his listening hat on," and nothing else, for a while. No problem solving, no discipline talk, or anything threatening, just a few minutes of listening. Using the core skills described in the last chapter, this unfolded quite rapidly, because he kept reflecting and summarizing how Joe was feeling and thinking as the story emerged. Eventually Joe said something like, "Yes, that's how I feel, you've got me."

The focusing process happened in stages, provided each time by the teacher, but with Joe's agreement. What started in the corridor as "How you are feeling about school?" narrowed down when Joe walked in, with the teacher suggesting that they talk about "how you might get on better in school." The horizon or change goal was set. Joe agreed.

"Useful talk" from a MI perspective really got going upon the platform of these two processes, engaging and focusing. As the account unfolds below, we will highlight nine guidelines for good practice in evoking (see Box 6.1 at the end of the chapter).

Guidelines for Evoking

Keep Working on Engagement and Avoid Arguing

Students who feel comfortable and engaged are more likely to be open and honest. What they say about change will more likely reflect what they really feel and want. This is why engagement is important. Otherwise a lot of students' language will be protective of their self-esteem, as in Joe's case, with phrases like, "Why should that teacher blame me, none of this is my fault" or "I don't need school, I got my own life." A calm, nonjudgmental attitude and acceptance of the student as a person (not necessarily of his or her behavior) will reap dividends and soften much of the hard language. Resist the temptation to meet arguments against change with counterarguments, like telling Joe "the real truth." Avoid arguments completely. Heated conversations can be fast paced, and the strain will affect both parties. Keep working on engagement. A calm and gentle pace will have an immediate impact on the quality of listening involved, and the progress made.

Accept Ambivalence as Normal

Joe probably has conflicting feelings about getting on better in school. Which student doesn't? It's just that some of the voices are louder and more habitually active than others, born of the bitter experience of not fitting in. A change conversation with Joe will make better progress if he feels the teacher is not taking sides, but accepts his feelings of ambivalence as normal. What are these voices of ambivalence? Consider Joe's voices for and against getting on better at school:

Against change (sustain talk)	*For change (change talk)*
"I'd rather not be here."	"Where else am I going to go?"
"I don't need those grades anyway."	"If I don't graduate, then what?"
"If I leave, at least I am free."	"I don't have many other options right now."
"I'm not putting up with this anymore."	"I've handled a lot in my life and I can meet challenges if I want to."

Notice the Change Talk, and Its Opposite, Sustain Talk

Joe's ambivalence is like a soup with mixed ingredients, with some flavors stronger than others. As a colleague once put it, it's like a committee meeting in the head, with sustain talk on one side of the table and change talk on the other. By having conversations with students, one gets better at noticing both change and sustain talk. Recognizing this language is one of the first steps in evoking. Consider the following shower of change talk and sustain talk from Joe:

TEACHER: So how do you feel about getting on better in school?

JOE: Well, I don't want to be expelled [Change talk], but it's not my fault. And why is it always me that those teachers pick on? I'm doing OK. [Sustain talk]

TEACHER: Some of this feels unfair to you. [Reflection]

JOE: No, all of it, that guy wound me up, he knew what he was doing so he got what he deserved. . . . I don't see why I should get into trouble, no way is that fair [Sustain talk], I don't need this hassle. [Change talk]

TEACHER: And you don't want to get into more trouble. [Reflection of change talk]

JOE: Yeah, I want to stay in school and keep to myself. [Change talk]

Contradictions shine out of Joe's statement above but remember the guideline about accepting ambivalence as normal. The apparently irrational and contradictory things that Joe says are not evidence for anything wrong, but merely the natural and common expressions of ambivalence we all feel when faced with daily decisions to change a behavior.

> *Recognizing sustain talk and change talk is one of the first steps in evoking.*

Noticing is a simple act, with much behind it. It's what happens when time stands still for a moment. The briefest of pauses in a conversation can allow this to happen, and it ideally goes both ways—you noticing the language that points to change, the student hearing himself say it and hopefully giving voice to what on balance he really wants. As he hears this, his resolve grows. Note that it can be hard for you to notice these things if your mind is distracted by trying to find a solution *for* the student.

Joe's teacher heard the contradictory voices for and against change, and gave them a chance to be aired, but he also kept his eye on the goal for Joe, getting on better in school.

> *It can be hard to notice these things if you're distracted by trying to find a solution for the student.*

Change Talk Varies in Strength

Change talk can vary in strength. The stronger it is, the more likely it signals readiness to change and predicts decision making. Notice the differences among these statements from students:

"I could stay in school."
"I want to stay in school."
"I've got to stay in school."
"I am definitely going to stay in school."

The first two of these statements are called "preparatory change talk." The latter two are much stronger and are called "commitment language."

Ask for Change Talk, with Carefully Worded Open Questions

You don't have to sit back and wait for change talk to emerge. You can ask for it. In situations where you don't hear any emerging spontaneously, it's probably your only option. Here are a few examples of questions that could be put to Joe:

"How might you get on better in school?"
"What makes sense to you? How can you keep out of trouble?"
"Where would you like to take yourself in the next year?"

The answers to all of these questions will be change talk, and their formulation and wording is worth taking a little time to get right. The student will appreciate this care. For example, with the first question, there's quite a big difference between "How *might* you get on better at school?" and "How *are* you going to get on better at school?" There's less pressure in the first one, which is more respectful of Joe's autonomy in a tight corner.

You don't have to sit back and wait for change talk to emerge. You can ask for it.

Ask Questions about Importance and Confidence

Questions about importance and confidence help to separate two sources of motivation to change: the "Why?" (importance) and the "How?" (confidence) of change. It's often wise to allow the energy in the why channel to grow before moving too quickly onto the how channel. Hence the following two questions:

"How important is it for you to stay on in school?"
"How confident do you feel about succeeding with this?"

There's no need to be too concerned about asking exactly the right question because if you are curious about finding out, someone like Joe will usually reveal where the challenge lies. Sometimes it is clear and distinct, other times it can be a mixture of importance and confidence. In the end, it's the very process of giving a student the opportunity to talk about change, free of judgment and interruption, that can make all the difference. Using MI, you merely create a cocoon around the two of you and accompany the student while he or she works it out.

A useful practical tool for exploring importance and confidence to change is a "ruler." Younger children especially enjoy exploring their motivation with numbers, an often-quick route to evoking change talk. You simply ask them "How important is it to . . . ?" or "How confident are do you feel succeeding at . . . ?" Then ask them to place themselves on the ruler—either a physical ruler or a line drawn on paper from 1 (no importance/confidence) to 10 (maximum importance/confidence). Next, you ask why they gave themselves that number and not a lower one (answer is change talk) or how their number might move up (more change talk).

Reflect Change Talk, Look for Opportunities to Affirm

Respond to change talk by reflecting it and look for chances to affirm as illustrated below.

> JOE: (*continuing from the above exchange*) Yeah, I want to stay in school and keep to myself. [Change talk]
>
> TEACHER: You know what you want and you don't want to get into more trouble. [Affirmation and reflection]
>
> JOE: Yeah, I still want to know how that guy is not expelled for what he did.
>
> TEACHER: You don't understand that and yet you also know what you want. [Reflection]
>
> JOE: I need to stay here because leaving will just get me into more trouble. [Stronger change talk]
>
> TEACHER: How might you get on better in school? [Open question]
>
> JOE: Like I say, keep to myself more. [Change talk]
>
> TEACHER: That might work for you. [Reflection]
>
> JOE: It might, but then there's these guys who just make trouble.

TEACHER: You might get sucked into a fight. [Reflection]

JOE: Yes, and I must step away and go solo until I calm down. [Change talk]

Joe's teacher used the one open question to firmly steer the focus toward change, but he mostly relied on reflecting, and it's here where there is the greatest room for Joe to breathe, resolve his ambivalence about staying in school, and develop a new perspective. It's also room for his teacher to breathe—he doesn't have to think of the next question he will ask. He has only to focus his attention on Joe and gently steer things with the thoughtfulness of his next reflection.

Over the last few decades we have identified through direct experience a number of finer technical nuances or strategies that will be of interest, and will certainly make for more efficient use of MI.

Using Reflections to Steer the Conversation

Sometimes, a student's change talk is so striking and lucid that you need do little else than stay with it, and not steer the conversation in any way. That's what the teacher did above when Joe said, "Yeah, I want to stay in school and keep to myself." He responded with a simple reflection, "You'd like to stay here."

Then there are times when it's useful to steer a little more, and you'll notice this above. Joe continued to express anger about another student ("Yeah, I still want to know how that guy is not expelled for what he did"). The teacher's reflection in response was "You don't understand that and yet you also know what you want." The first part of the reflection acknowledged how Joe felt, but the second part steered the conversation back to the change talk and what Joe wanted for himself. Joe replied by affirming his desire to stay in school.

Using Understated Reflections

The closer students get to the heart of their ambivalence, the more sensitive they become to pressure, and the more they will appreciate having the autonomy to make up their own minds. They want to give their own words to their feelings. For a student facing expulsion, you might want to say, "You definitely don't want to be expelled." But it would be more effective to say, "You *might* not find expulsion so easy." The second reflection gives the student more freedom to express his feelings.

Using Double-Sided Reflections

As described in Chapter 5, a double-sided reflection restates both sides of ambivalence. These can be very useful with ambivalence so common in change conversation. Consider this:

> JOE: I just don't know, I don't want to be on the street but this place sucks and I hate it because those teachers . . .
>
> TEACHER: You don't like it here and you don't want to leave school either.

Consider the *ordering* of the above double-sided reflection. How might Joe respond if the order were reversed to: "You don't want to leave school and you don't like it here either?" He will probably respond to the second half, the last thing the teacher said, in this case with more sustain talk. The teacher, however, ended with the change side of the ambivalence: ". . . you don't want to leave school. . . . " This sets Joe up to talk more about why he doesn't want to leave school, more change talk.

Allow the Student's Response to Guide You

When first learning to use reflection it can feel overwhelming, such is the array of possibilities for listening with care. Student statements can seem confusing or contradictory, and there you are trying to judge the strength of change talk, or wondering exactly how to frame your next reflection. There's a lot going on. You can get distracted by thinking too much and lose the flow. It can feel like you are losing control of the conversation. The inclination to take control can rise up, but if you do that, it will block the evoking process at precisely the point where the student might be about to break through into clear thinking.

It takes restraint to follow the guideline, "Reflect the change talk." Yet with practice it can approach what a colleague once said about her skill development: "I use reflections with ease, knowing that they help the student to work out why and how they might change." Inside that comment sits a guideline worth noting: if the student seems to be responding positively, and is immersed in why or how he or she might change, it's a signal that you have done something useful. In this sense the student is your best teacher. If all else fails, consider being frank about your feelings and ask the student what she or he thinks.

Use Summaries That Capture the Change Talk and Are Forward-Looking

In the last chapter the core skill of summarizing was described as useful for pulling together part of a conversation and for changing direction. Here, in the practice of MI, another very useful function of a summary emerges: it allows you to capture the change talk. In that exchange with Joe, he would have heard the change talk as he expressed it, heard it in the teacher's reflection, and could have then heard it for a third time in the summary. The energy for and commitment to change builds for Joe as he hears back his own language. You are best advised to produce this summary by using the students' words as much as possible, to use "you" when referring to their positive motivations, and leave out superfluous language like, "One of the things I hear you say is . . . ." Crisper, well-crafted summaries produce clearer student reactions.

> *A summary allows you to pull together and capture the change talk.*

A colleague once described her use of MI like this: "I ask, listen, log, ask listen log, ask listen log, then I summarize what's in the log."[1] She meant that she was making mental notes of the person's *motivations and strengths* during the conversation about change. Then she used a summary to pull the notes together and present them to the person. Start with something like this, "Can I summarize what you have said so far?" If summarizing while evoking is like presenting a bouquet of flowers to the person, then you don't want to include too many weeds (the sustain talk).

Ask a Key Question about Action

In the moment after producing a summary, you hold the young person in a thoughtful frame of mind. If the summary has captured the dilemma, he or she might move forward, often saying something like, "Yes, that's how I feel." Then there is often a valuable silence, and you can simply ask a key question, for example, "Where does this leave you now?"

Questions like that are effectively invitations and are best worded to maximize autonomy and avoid a confrontational tone. The following key question, for example, is confrontational, clumsy, and could elicit defensiveness: "So what are you going to do about this?" A more neutral question is "What do you think you might do?" This gives the student the autonomy that's essential for steering a new course.

---

[1] Thanks to Dr. Nina Gobat for this suggestion.

Change Happens Naturally; Try Not to Get in the Way

It's worth remembering that change often occurs outside of a conversation and is a natural process. Not getting in the way of that process can be more helpful than we realize. In Joe's case, the discussion did not take too long. Engagement was key, and his teacher made sure he did not get in the way. The answer was inside Joe, and the teacher created the conditions for Joe to release the energy and motivation that were already there and enabled him to move forward. Change talk emerged naturally, a bit like just removing a block or two rather than every brick in the dam. A summary list of the guidelines for evoking change can be found in Box 6.1.

Beneath the details about evoking in this chapter sits a foundation of guiding well known to teachers, administrators, and other school staff. In this sense, learning MI is merely continuing a professional journey already begun. It's also often a matter of what you leave out of the conversation, or what you don't do. The MI conversation omits judgments about motivation and behavior, and noisy efforts to persuade or to push the student toward change. Instead, it encourages the student to face her or his choices bravely and move toward a decision to change. In asking students "What might you do?," you invite them to take the next step—planning change—the subject of the next chapter.

BOX 6.1. Guidelines for Evoking Change Talk

1. Keep working on engagement and avoid arguing.

2. Accept ambivalence as normal.

3. Notice the change talk, and its opposite, sustain talk.

4. Ask for change talk, with carefully worded open questions.

5. Reflect the change talk with a keen eye on affirmation.

6. Allow the student's response to guide you.

7. Use summaries that are forward-looking and capture the change talk.

8. Ask key questions about action.

9. Change happens naturally—try not to get in the way.

Planning Changes

Plans are nothing; planning is everything.
—*Dwight D. Eisenhower*

Planning flows from and overlaps with evoking. Where evoking is mostly about whether to change and why, planning is about what and how. Educators are well versed in how to develop actions plans. The discussion below therefore focuses on how MI can be woven into routine educational planning and so work *with* a student's motivation, rather than against it. As the chapter unfolds a series of 10 guidelines for using MI for planning will emerge (see Box 7.2 at the end of the chapter). We begin with the transition from evoking to planning and then turn to making a change plan.

As Evoking Merges with Planning

Demonstrate Acceptance of Continued Ambivalence

A student apparently wants to change, yet can't see how to make this happen. Notice the word "but" in the following:

"I want to get on top of this subject, but how?"
"I can see that I really need to do this, but . . . "
"Yeah, OK for some, but I try and I keep failing."

It's in the nature of trial-and-error learning that ambivalence creeps back, especially in the dip of failure. It's a natural reaction for the student to waver about the importance of change, the confidence to achieve it, or both. The more complex the change, the louder and more fearful these voices might become, and the more important it is to use core skills like reflection and affirmation to help the student reaffirm the value of the goal, and gather the courage to try and try again. Paying attention to the language of change allows you to read its signals and makes the journey as a whole much less bumpy.

Notice Stronger Change Talk, Affirm It, and Reflect It

As someone crosses the bridge to planning, you will notice an increase in change talk along with a decrease in its opposite, sustain talk. The ratio between the two starts to shift.

The strength of the change talk also increases. For example, "I might" becomes "I can." "I'll probably get to do that" becomes "I very much want to." It takes just a moment or two to use reflection and affirmation in reply. This can validate students' feelings of competence in regulating themselves and give them hope, lifting them immensely.

Hope Breeds Success

Research suggests that hope breeds success (see Miller & Rollnick, 2013), and hope can be evoked from within the person. A good relationship, feeling understood, and feeling affirmed can all support this process. As we have said elsewhere, affirming a person's strengths is a way of bolstering hope and confidence when that person is short on it. Box 7.1 provides an example.

Avoid Jumping Ahead of the Student's Readiness

Avoid taking over the planning process, and unwittingly disempowering the student. Self-determination theory (Ryan & Deci, 2000) helps to explain this challenge: a student will learn and change if three basic needs are met: for autonomy ("This is my action plan"), for relatedness ("It's helpful talking with you about this"), and for competence ("Here are some things I might succeed with").

A common mistake (born probably of frustration) is jumping ahead of the student's readiness. This can elicit further uncertainty and backtracking, for example, "No, I'm not sure about that because. . . . "

BOX 7.1. Evoking Hope with a 9-Year-Old: An Exercise

Emily was a quiet and diligent child with troubles at home, and it showed in her school work. Her teacher asked her whether she wanted to do an exercise for a few minutes. When Emily agreed, the teacher showed her a list of 20 positive attributes with pictures alongside, and asked her to find five that described her best. The attributes included things like "playful," "energetic," "intelligent," "healthy," "caring," and so on. Emily was engaged. As Emily told the teacher the attributes she had selected, the teacher listened and gave her a moment to expand on each one. The teacher asked open questions about how Emily expressed the attributes in her daily life, and reflected her answers. The teacher then asked an open question that clearly evoked change talk. "How can these ones you have chosen help you with your school work?"

A statement like this is a signal to reengage using core skills and clarify readiness to change. That is what the teacher below does in talking to a student about being more organized with school books, at home, and at school:

TEACHER: Maybe using a new filing system might help? [Jumping ahead]

STUDENT: No, I'm not sure about that because I don't know how to use things like files for my papers.

TEACHER: You want to be more organized but something is slowing you down. [Reflection]

STUDENT: I don't know—it just feels difficult.

TEACHER: I wonder what small things could help you get started, so it does not feel so difficult?

Even if a student seems more than ready to change it can be helpful to double-check this by asking a few open questions about why this is the case. This important step elicits the kind of change talk that can galvanize the commitment the student will no doubt need as the planning unfolds.

In summary, while planning follows from evoking, evoking doesn't end once planning begins. It continues and merges with the planning process.

Ask about Readiness and Respond Using Core Skills, Particularly Affirmation

If you are not sure about readiness, test the water. Simply ask a student how ready she or he is to change, with an open question like "How ready do you feel to [make this change]?"

> Evoking doesn't end once planning begins.

Making a Change Plan

Our attention here is on how a task is to be carried out with the student, not just on what you do. The MI conversation has the power to get the best out of whatever system of change planning is being used. We will continue highlighting key guidelines as the chapter unfolds.

Ask Open Questions That Focus on Competence, Choice, and Specificity

Making a change plan is a process that seldom goes in a straight line. Two things seem to happen with successful plans: one is that they get more concrete; some say the more specific the better. The other is that the student's sense of competence about success grows. Open questions are useful for eliciting specificity and competence. The wording of the following questions can help pull the best out of a student:

"What's going to work best for you?"
"What one or two things will work best for you?"
"Of the options you have, which one would suit you the best?"
"What choices can you see here?"
"How exactly might you go about that?"

> Making a change plan seldom goes in a straight line.

Gather Choices and Encourage Ownership of Solution(s)

Younger students and those who need more active support respond well to a structured process for gathering choices. In brainstorming, students create a list of possible ideas, verbally or on paper, while suspending all judgments about the ideas generated. Some students can work with just a couple of choices; others need a longer list. Adding ideas of your own can also be helpful if delivered in a way that still gives the choice back to the student.

Follow-up questions can be used to translate intentions into specific actions, for example, "How exactly will you do this, and when?"

Evoke and Reinforce Commitment Language

Planning by asking questions alone can leave the student waiting passively for the next input from you. The decision about what will work best is inside the student despite the uncertainty about which way to go. This is why it's important to notice and reinforce change talk with reflection, particularly commitment language. As we described in Chapter 6, commitment language is the strongest type of change talk, but it too can vary in strength.

Notice how the strength of the change talk goes from weak to strong commitment in these three examples, in each case followed by a reflection designed to reinforce it:

Weak commitment language

STUDENT: I could do that, for sure.

ADMINISTRATOR: It's something you might try. [Reflection]

Moderate commitment language

STUDENT: I am going to see if that works.

ADMINISTRATOR: You've come to a decision about that. [Reflection]

Strong commitment language

STUDENT: I'm doing that tomorrow morning at 9:30 A.M., I promise.

ADMINISTRATOR: It's clear for you now and you are determined to do it. [Reflection]

Each of the administrator's reflections will evoke more commitment language. Together with affirmation, they cement further the student's determination and the potential of a change plan.

Encourage Students to Share Decisions with Others and to Keep a Record of Success

Conversation is limited. Action happens out there in the social environment. It's where trial and error unfolds. Talking about what kind of support will be helpful can carry a lot of weight, and behavior change researchers have shone a spotlight on what promotes or hinders change. They found that a more public commitment to the decision, that is, telling others or at least someone else, is linked to better outcome (Barber & Crisp, 1995; Longabaugh, Wirtz, Zweben, & Stout, 1998). In addition, if it's realistic for the student, "self-monitoring" or keeping a record of success, reinforces progress (Kanfer, 1970; Safren et al., 2001).

Help Students to View Slips as Opportunities to Learn

Change is cyclical. "Mistakes" are part of the natural change process, the sometimes inevitable slipping and sliding back that sits at the center of learning. One of us received a salutatory lesson on just this from a 2-year-old: he finally succeeded with a task, then instead of repeating the successful move, he repeated the wrong one, and then did it again. Slipping and failing are essential for learning to take place, and it's helpful if the person remains engaged and focused. Much in this book is about helping you do that with a student. Help students to view slipping and sliding as opportunities to learn.

> *Help students to view slipping as an opportunity to learn.*

Help Students with the Gentle Anticipation of Barriers to Success

Helpful planning often involves the gentle anticipation of barriers. The core skills of MI can be invaluable aids to exploring these: ask an open question that raises the subject; use reflection to clarify the student's concerns; and particularly use affirmation to encourage persistence and the generation of new ideas for overcoming the barrier.

The counselor in the conversation below helps a student anticipate barriers to being more organized at home and at school:

COUNSELOR: I wonder what small things could help you get started, so it does not feel so difficult? [Open question]

STUDENT: Maybe I could tidy up one part of my room, and call it my school space. [Change talk]

COUNSELOR: That's something you could do to make a start. [Reflection]

STUDENT: Yes, I could do that. [Change talk]

COUNSELOR: I wonder, what might get in the way of you succeeding with this? [Question about barriers]

STUDENT: Lots of things, like when I get home, I just want to relax and use my computer, not tidy my desk up. [Sustain talk]

COUNSELOR: You can see this as a challenge that might get in the way. [Reflection]

STUDENT: Oh yeah, I'd need to make a decision and go for it. [Change talk]

COUNSELOR: And you are quite close to making that decision. [Reflection, a guess]

STUDENT: Yeah, I could do it this afternoon. [Change talk]

COUNSELOR: You've got determination in you, and maybe today is the day. [Reflection, affirmation]

STUDENT: I think so.

This chapter started with a note about how the evoking process merges with that of planning. Seen in this light, planning is not something separate from evoking, but simply a conversation about the what and how of change, in which the spirit and core skills of MI can be used to good effect.

Box 7.2 contains a summary of the main points to emerge in this chapter.

And Giving Advice?

Input from an educator in the planning process is best captured by the word "suggestion" rather than the giving of advice. Giving a student advice carries the risk of undermining his or her choice and autonomy. It's a fine line between advice and a suggestion to consider a possibility. How to walk this line in situations where advice is clearly called for is the subject of the next chapter.

BOX 7.2. Guidelines for Planning with Students

1. Demonstrate acceptance of continued ambivalence.

2. Notice the stronger change talk, affirm it, and reflect it.

3. Avoid jumping ahead of the student's readiness.

4. Ask about readiness and respond using core skills, particularly affirmation.

5. Ask open questions that focus on competence, choice, and specificity.

6. Gather choices and encourage ownership of solution(s).

7. Evoke and reinforce commitment language.

8. Encourage students to share decisions with others and keep a record of success.

9. Help students to view slips as opportunities to learn.

10. Help students with the gentle anticipation of barriers to success.

8

The MI Approach to Giving Information and Advice

> After all, when you seek advice from someone
> it's certainly not because you want them to
> give it. You just want them to be there while
> you talk to yourself.
>
> —*Terry Prachett*

This opening quotation from the British writer and raconteur Terry Pratchett captures the value of change talk: sometimes when you ask for advice you find yourself talking aloud about how to solve a problem, with the other person more or less giving you the time and space to do this. Enabling students to do this with you in the maelstrom of school life is certainly not easy, but it is a key message of this book. Hearing repetitive calls to change from the outside unwittingly distracts students from working things out for themselves.

Imagine a survey on this question: "What percentage of time in school is spent on passing information to students, in the form of instruction, advice, presenting new material, giving feedback, and so on?" Some might say it's a dull question, so uniformly high would the percentage be, because that's what classes are all about sometimes. Then what about this question: "How skillful an activity is this?" The answers will be much more diverse. Some will point to the fact that much of information delivery is simple, routine, and necessary. Others will highlight the starting point for this chapter, pointing perhaps to a moment when a student really learned, noting that on some occasions informing and advising, done skillfully, enhances learning, motivation, and change. Most will probably agree that how it is done makes a difference. Information imparted as a tired and dry ritual will be unrewarding for all involved, and this can happen with even the most carefully planned lesson. Sydney J. Harris, the renowned journalist, once apparently said, "The two words 'information' and 'communication' are often used interchangeably but they are quite different things. Information is giving out, communication is getting through."

Our aim in this chapter is to highlight circumstances where MI can make informing and advising more effective.

The Elicit–Provide–Elicit Framework

The link between skillful informing in education and in MI is no coincidence. William R. Miller and his colleagues (Miller, Sovereign, & Krege, 1988) in New Mexico were trying to educate people about the dangers of problem drinking by giving them their test results and helping them decide whether or not to change. Miller and colleagues decided to first ask people what they would most like to know before giving them information; then they provided the information without interpretation. Finally they used their listening skills to find out what sense each person made of it all. On its own, this led to changes in behavior. It was the inspiration behind the elicit–provide–elicit framework.

The three steps in the framework, when used in a school environment, are:

1. *Elicit* what the student knows or would like to know.
2. *Provide* information tailored to the student's needs.
3. *Elicit* what sense the student makes of the information.

This framework is notable for what it does *not* contain: the provider of information refrains from telling the student what to do, and avoids telling him or her how to interpret the information. Instead, MI skills are used to evoke from students what sense they make of it.

What you don't do is as important as what you do do. Pausing, for example, allows the information to "sink in" and allows new questions to arise for the receiver.

In practice, the three phases—elicit–provide–elicit—often happen in a cycle. The conversation swings between eliciting and providing in a fluid two-way exchange. Core skills like open questions and reflection are used in the eliciting phase to draw out and extend the student's understanding.

Three Basic Needs: Autonomy, Relatedness, and Competence

Beneath the surface of successful information provision is a person whose needs are met in some way. The basic needs described in self-determination theory (Ryan & Deci, 2000) are also helpful here. The theory posits that a person will learn and change if three needs are met, for autonomy, relatedness, and competence.

These concepts come to life if we consider the following provision of information. A teacher says:

> "You've got most of it right, but go back to your desk now. There's a problem with your understanding 'a' and 'b.' I have told you before that they don't go together, and that if you look at it another way, you'll see the difference."

The above teacher is not engaged with the student (relatedness), questions his or her competence ("I have told you before . . . "), and has not reinforced autonomy in any meaningful way. The likelihood is that learning has been depressed. Information giving is seen as pressing the information down into the student's head, putting the lid on, and learning will, or should, take place.

The student's three core needs might be better met, and the outcome be more favorable, if the teacher said something like this:

> "You've done well here. It's almost right. See what you think about 'a' and 'b' not going together, and let me know how I can help. When you go back to your desk, see if you can work it out, and give me a shout if you need help, OK?"

Competence has been highlighted ("You've done well here"); the student has been given some choices about how to proceed (autonomy); and the relaxed "give me a shout . . . " approaches the learner's need for relatedness with the teacher. These three concepts highlight the ingredients of a guiding style introduced in Chapter 3. It is coming alongside someone with expertise while he or she uses his or her expertise to search for a solution, the heart of skillful teaching. Even without using a framework like elicit–provide–elicit, this teacher has successfully provided information that is more likely to promote learning and change.

Common Scenarios

The scenarios below illustrate applications using the elicit–provide–elicit framework described above.

Providing New Material

Effective teaching involves presenting new material in a lively way that has a group of students engaged and curious. When this doesn't happen, it's all too easy either to blame the students ("They just aren't motivated to learn") or perhaps the subject ("This part of the curriculum isn't very interesting"). This was precisely the kind of attribution of blame to external forces that struck William Miller as oversimplified when he first developed MI: maybe, he thought, it has something to do with my conversation style?

The elicit–provide–elicit framework helps ensure that providers of information keep to a style that maximizes their ability to engage students and promote change. For example, before *providing* information, is there an opportunity, even a very brief one, for first *eliciting* the expectations and interest of students? Students can be asked questions like, "What do you know about . . . ?" or "Who can tell me something about . . . ?" Similarly, once the information has been provided, is there time to *elicit* their views about what the information means for them?

Giving Feedback

The most common scenario for giving feedback is presenting test results, either individually or in a group. Beforehand most students are wondering what their outcomes will be. The opening *elicit* phase of the strategy helps them express this reality openly, either in a few moments or in a more structured way, by eliciting their expectations with questions like "What concerns do you have about these results?" or "What would you most like to know and why?" The results are then provided, and the teacher returns to eliciting, with questions that open the door to using MI like "How do you feel about this result?" or "How would you like to do better next time?" Even quite young children can express these fears and aspirations. Answers to the question about doing better next time usually take the form of change talk (see Chapter 6). Pausing to give time to this kind of talk can enhance motivation and reap dividends.

The elicit–provide–elicit strategy can also be used to guide feedback about behavior. For example, a teacher or administrator might sit with a student to discuss a problem behavior and start by *eliciting* his or her story, or even expectations about the outcome. After *providing* information about the school's view, a final discussion could turn to *eliciting* the student's ideas about the implications of his or her behavior and how to avoid this problem in the future.

Giving Advice That Respects Autonomy, Competence, and Relatedness

Advice is information with a steer, or a sting, depending on how you

> *Advice is information with a steer, or a sting, depending on how you give it.*

give it. It's a message about what the student should or could do, and the skillfulness of delivery might make all the difference between a blank look and much keener uptake.

It's difficult to find research evidence on the effect of skillfulness in advice giving and its outcome. The guidelines below rely unashamedly on our own experience, with attention to students' basic needs for autonomy, competence, and relatedness. There is an important difference between a genuine suggestion and an instruction. The former helps the student choose what suits her or him, the latter leaves little choice. These guidelines can be adapted to suit your circumstances.

- *Engage* the student if possible before giving advice.
- *Ask permission.* This is not only a matter of being polite, but also of genuinely giving the student freedom to say, "No thank you." For example, you could say something like, "I am getting an idea about what you might do, and I wonder whether you'd like to hear it, or would you rather I leave this up to you to work out for yourself?"
- *Offer choices* wherever possible: "You could do 'x,' or you could consider 'y.'" Choice promotes autonomy, while also preventing the trap of offering one idea at a time, only to be met with "No, that wouldn't work" or "I've already tried that." You genuinely want the person to feel that he or she has the freedom to make his or her own good decisions. Use language that reflects this attitude: "It's up to you"; "I am not sure what will really suit

you—that's your decision." Minimizing language aids this process: "You might . . . "; or "You might think about . . . "; "You could . . . " or "A little. . . ."

- *Elicit reaction.* Offering some time to allow the student to absorb the advice could be valuable and then ask what the student thinks about what you said.

Some students might want or need more direct advice than suggested above, in which case you might simply offer a suggestion and make sure to note that they still have a choice about whether to follow it or not.

Choice promotes autonomy.

Let the Student Guide You

Straightforward and routine information delivery has its place, as does information delivered skillfully to promote learning and change. Noticing when to use which one is itself a marker of skillfulness. Blank looks in students might be a signal to change from a routine approach to one that is more evocative.

Students' blank looks call for switching to a more evocative style.

Information that nurtures curiosity lies at the heart of learning and MI. Shared curiosity about the meaning and relevance of information provides the ideal platform for MI. When the student feels safe enough to receive information and wonder about the way ahead, change talk will emerge, and this takes you into the orbit of MI, where core skills to elicit more change talk can open up the path to change. The tougher the problem facing you and the student, the softer might be the style needed to help him or her face it.

IN PRACTICE

This part of the book illustrates what MI might look and feel like in and around the classroom, corridors, and other places in school. The idea is not to cover every technical detail, but rather to capture a range of scenarios in which MI might offer support to improve conversations and their outcomes.

In these four chapters the style and skills described in Part I are illustrated in context, with one caveat in mind: there's no one correct way to speak with students, and MI is not an end in itself, merely a way of widening your skill base. Our goal here is to show how the skills of MI can improve conversation outcomes in the short run and save time in the long run.

The table on the next page maps out the chapters in this part, and will help you to access both the topics and elements of MI of greatest interest to you. We also address the common question of "Does MI work with younger students?" in each of these chapters to follow.

Overview of Part II Chapters

Scenario	Topic	Illustrating
Chapter 9: Behavior, Behavior, Behavior		
9.1. *That Kid Is Always Late*: 12-year-old girl (p. 75)	An everyday problem behavior	Three communication styles
9.2. *Misbehaving and Going Around in Circles*: 8-year-old boy (p. 79)	Multiple, interrelated behavioral problems	Two brief conversations showing engagement and the spirit of MI
9.3. *Preventing a Fight in the Hall*: 16-year-old girl (p. 82)	A heated exchange between two students	How engagement can diffuse anger and how evoking solutions from a student can lead to progress
Chapter 10: Learning		
10.1. *I Just Don't Get It!*: 15-year-old girl (p. 88)	A student struggles with math	Brief conversations to engage and evoke solutions from the student using the elicit–provide–elicit and ruler strategies
10.2. *Students Never Come to Class Prepared*: 16- to 17-year-olds (p. 92)	Presenting a reading assignment to the whole class	Use of elicit–provide–elicit strategy and reflection to limit discord and collective resistance to an assignment
10.3. *You're All Facing Change: Let's Discuss This*: 14-year-olds (p. 97)	A lesson conducted using MI skills	Using MI spirit and skills to evoke classwide discussion where students feel heard, happy to share their ideas, and learn from each other in facing change
Chapter 11: Personal Development		
11.1. *I'm So Torn*: 17-year-old girl (p. 103)	Ambivalence about peer relationships	MI and resolving ambivalence
11.2. *He's Got Potential, but . . .* : 15-year-old boy (p. 107)	Helping a student to look forward and plan	How acceptance and affirmation evoke change talk about plans that make sense to the student
11.3. *Just a Bump in the Road?*: 17-year-old boy (p. 110)	In trouble with the police	Shifting between the three communication styles to come alongside a student, elicit his or her aspirations, and clarify what will happen next

(continued)

Overview of Part II Chapters (*continued*)

Scenario	Topic	Illustrating
Chapter 12: Working with Families		
12.1. *Making a Short Telephone Conversation Count*: 9-year-old boy (p. 117)	Your child's behavior in class	Developing a partnership and evoking solutions in an efficient manner while avoiding the blaming trap
12.2. *Report Card: Unhappy Student, Frustrated Parent*: 10-year-old girl (p. 121)	Difficult three-way conversation	Using core skills to find agreement about the way ahead
12.3. *Angry Parent: "I'm Very Upset with This Situation"*: No age specified (p. 124)	A series of angry statements by parents	Different replies, different outcomes

9

Behavior, Behavior, Behavior

We are not tinkers who merely patch and mend
what is broken . . . we must be watchmen,
guardians of the life and the health of our
generation, so that stronger and more able
generations may come after.
—*Dr. Elizabeth Blackwell*

There's a long list of reasons why behavioral problems arise in
schools. The world outside is a huge influence, and the environment
within the school can also contribute. Clearly, the ability and will to
self-regulate and problem-solve varies across students. Consider this
scenario:

"Bruce is constantly blowing up; if it is not with a teacher, it is
with another student. He loses it and when confronted he blames
others for causing the trouble. So then in the end he's told he
must bring in a parent, who always seems to be at wit's end. We
give him consequences and ultimatums and he still keeps misbehaving. I just can't see what's in it for him; he just gets into more
trouble."

MI can certainly help with a fresh approach to this kind of challenge. What it doesn't involve is labeling or blaming this young man,

or focusing exclusively on tighter and tighter control over his behavior. You could compel students to stay at their desks at all times, march them out in lines into the playground, use police to monitor them, and run a regime so tough that behavioral problems are minimized, but at what cost? Beneath the surface of such a scenario are a few well-known truths: discipline and setting boundaries for children have a very clear place in education *and* they are not enough; similarly, fear induction and punishment aren't necessarily the only or the best ways to promote behavior change. Something will be missing. Put bluntly, students have *needs* that call for attention, and there are few teachers, counselors, administrators, or coaches who went into their professions without wanting to help students meet them. The most effective behavioral interventions are probably those that use a range of approaches simultaneously, and are able to address students' needs.

> *Fear and punishment aren't necessarily the best ways to promote behavior change.*

The Contribution of MI

Here are two reasons why MI might help with behavioral problems:

1. MI focuses simultaneously on behavior change *and* the wider personal needs of the student.
2. MI is particularly suited to tough problems. It originated in addiction treatment, a setting in which very difficult and life-threatening conversations about behavior change took place. Counter to popular beliefs at the time, it turned out that really hard problems could be tackled using a softer style, free of blaming, labeling, and inducing fear. Teachers and other school personnel face a very similar challenge.

Efforts to change behavior inevitably involve conversation. This chapter illustrates how MI can be used in three different scenarios where behavior change is the focus. Each scenario begins with a summary that describes the scenario and identifies the skills that it will illustrate. What all the scenarios have in common is that the teacher focuses on the student as a person, not just on his or her behavior. This allows the teacher to effect change in both attitude and behavior because the students take ownership of the changes.

Scenario 9.1. *"That Kid Is Always Late"*

Scenario

A teacher decides to have a word with a 12-year-old girl after she came slouching into class, almost like she's walking on air, not at all bothered about being late. She sat down like she was doing the world a favor by being there. She had a late pass from the office. The frequency of her lateness is the problem. Punishment doesn't seem to work. What next?

What the Scenario Illustrates

The three communication styles: Instead of launching into warning and scolding, the teacher uses a broader range of styles, starting with following, then guiding, and then finally using a directing style to clarify boundaries. This scenario provides examples of the three communication styles with an emphasis on MI's foundation *guiding* style. Later examples will illustrate MI itself more fully.

Setting Your Sights

Something is up with this student. Focusing only on setting limits and consequences has not worked thus far. *Engagement* might help to begin with, using a following style with open questions and reflections. These skills will help the teacher connect with the student and show her that the teacher wants to understand what's going on for her. Continuity is important. The teacher probably won't try to solve this problem in one conversation.

Yet the teacher doesn't want only to engage. The conversation will also need focus and direction. Can the student be encouraged to solve the problem herself? That's where a guiding style might be useful. Setting clear behavioral limits will be important, but can this be done on the platform of engagement, without threatening the student and making her feel scared? A following style is used to begin with.

Traps to Avoid

The righting reflex: The teacher needs to avoid reliance on the righting reflex—the tendency to see a problem and solve it immediately for the student (see Chapter 1). Usually this involves a directing style, which is essential for running a class and a school, but limited. It needs to be thoughtfully combined with the other styles, guiding and following. The teacher needs to take advantage of the powerful influence of engaging first with a student.

In Practice

The teacher has only a few minutes after class.

> TEACHER: I see that you find it hard to get into class on time, and I just wanted to have a quiet word with you about this. Can I ask you what is going on here? [Asked with genuine curiosity and a quiet firmness; following style initiated]
>
> STUDENT: Dunno. I suppose I'm just late (*no eye contact*).
>
> TEACHER: You're not able to get here on time. [Reflection]
>
> STUDENT: Don't know.
>
> TEACHER: You could get here but there's other things going on. [Another reflection, a guess]
>
> STUDENT: No. I just don't get here, that's all.
>
> TEACHER: You don't really feel like being here. [Another guess]
>
> STUDENT: (*Looks up for the first time.*) No, I don't.
>
> TEACHER: I don't mean to be too nosy, but can I ask you why?
>
> STUDENT: I just don't like it here.
>
> TEACHER: The thought of coming to school is not nice for you. [Reflection]
>
> STUDENT: Yes, that's right.

Commentary

Only a *following style* has been used thus far, and it took quite a few reflections to get to how the student really felt. The teacher's goal has been to do nothing but search for understanding, and to convey this desire to the student. Two open questions and four reflections have led to the student saying, "Yes, that's right." This is what we mean by "rapid engagement." It often happens when the sole focus is on engagement early on. The faster the engagement, the faster the progress! This connection is fragile, and whatever else is said afterward, engagement needs to be maintained and enhanced. That's why the core skill of reflection forms the glue for all to follow.

The teacher next switches style to a *guiding style*—this is about change, about evoking from the student why and how she might

> *The faster the engagement, the faster the progress.*

change. Setting limits using a *directing style* will come toward the end of the conversation.

TEACHER: What can you or I do to make this easier for you? [An open question about change]

STUDENT: Nothing really.

TEACHER: There's things going on here that you just don't like. [Reflection]

STUDENT: Yes, that's right. I hate this place.

TEACHER: Making it easier for you might be difficult. [Another reflection]

STUDENT: Yeah.

TEACHER: And coming in late? Anything you can do to sort that out?

STUDENT: Maybe.

TEACHER: You'll see if you can be on time. [Reflection]

STUDENT: Yeah, maybe.

TEACHER: It doesn't feel easy but you might make an effort. [Reflection]

STUDENT: Yeah.

Commentary

Only a very brief switch to a *directing style* is now necessary.

TEACHER: I guess you know that I need to run the class and this means everyone being in on time. I wanted to have a quiet word with you because I can see you are not happy when you walk in, and would you mind if we had another chat some other time?

STUDENT: No, fine.

TEACHER: I'm here to help, so don't hesitate to ask.

STUDENT: Yeah, thanks.

Commentary

In the above dialogue the student starts to say how she might change. More conversations are necessary, but this lays the foundations for the student acting to change in the future.

In this example there are reasonably clear differences in the tone and purpose of each of the three styles. Following is used to understand with a focus on student needs; guiding is used to help the person consider change, face forward, and say why or how this might come about; directing is used to communicate clearly about boundaries and consequences.

You might well question the last few lines that illustrate directing. After all, the teacher never even spelled out what the consequences might be if the student came in late next time. "That would never work in my setting," you might say. There's no one correct way to have a conversation. However, having established engagement and some understanding of how this young girl feels, the teacher could undo this good work by ending the conversation with what could be seen as a threat. The student probably knows what the consequences are. A choice was made to show some trust, knowing that if or when there is a repetition of lateness, the consequences can be made perfectly clear at that time. The success of this little exchange lies in part on the teacher's next move.

Across Ages

For younger students it may make most sense to reach out to parents with concerns about student attendance or tardiness. Certainly MI can play a role in those conversations with parents too, as we describe in Chapter 12. For older students a similar style to what we have outlined here would be helpful, although your curiosity about possible barriers to student attendance would likely expand to such areas as responsibilities at home, peer influences, and how students see school helping them (or not) with where they are heading in life. Making explicit that change is the student's choice can further engagement and reduce discord.

Scenario 9.2. "Misbehaving and Going Around in Circles"

Scenario

An 8-year-old boy repeatedly has to go to the office for misbehavior. He is just back from a suspension due to a fight in gym class. He has earned a reputation for having a short fuse and frequently creates problems. He gets up from his seat frequently, shouts out to others during quiet time, and touches and pushes others. Most of his teachers agree that he is able to keep up academically when he applies himself. He does not hold grudges, is socially outgoing, and responds well to positive attention. A teacher decides to take a fresh approach to tackle an old problem: disruptive behavior.

What the Scenario Illustrates

The use of MI's core skills (OARS) with a younger student: Simpler language, focusing on the here and now. The conversation is abbreviated in parts to avoid repetition and to focus on MI itself, where the evoking process is evident in brief conversations that will continue in the months to come.

Setting Your Sights

With firm and clear consequences in place for a student like this (detention, suspension, and summer school), is there some way in which a new page can be turned, using skillful conversation?

The teacher decides to engage, convey patience, and instill a belief that things can change. It's a remarkable truth that many adults can vividly recall a teacher who really believed in their ability to change and to learn from their mistakes. The teacher below is a bit like a sailor helping the student to learn how to move the boat in a more fruitful direction. In the conversation, the teacher does not solve every problem, but uses MI skills to help the student do some of this work for himself. She notices *change talk* like spotting a shift in wind direction.

Traps to Avoid

Ignoring a change window: Opportunities to promote change arise frequently, unexpectedly, often in times of crisis. A small window has opened on this boy's return from suspension, and if ignored there is every risk that he will be thrown back into the very circumstances that failed to encourage change in the first place. If the teacher perseveres with the same approach, the student will most likely return to old patterns of behavior.

Negative judgment: This is hard to avoid in a student who seems to have "multiple problems" almost written on his forehead. Progress might depend on avoiding this trap, and viewing the boy as a young person with potential, not just as a student with problems.

Blaming: Blaming someone evokes resistance, denial, and low motivation to change. It's incompatible with a student to recognizing and accepting the need to change behavior. MI provides the conversational tools to recognize a blaming pattern and to respond in a different way.

Blaming evokes resistance.

In Practice

In the corridor, the teacher's greeting is warm and accepting of the boy. They agree to speak as the day unfolds. During class, the teacher approaches the student's desk.

TEACHER: I see that you did the assignment. Another example of you working hard. [Affirmation]

STUDENT: Yup. Actually, my mother made me, but it was pretty easy.

TEACHER: When you are focused, you get things done. [Affirmation]

STUDENT: Yeah, well it was boring being at home with no friends around.

TEACHER: Having friends around is something you really like about school. [Reflection]

STUDENT: I like being with my friends, it's more fun.

TEACHER: You have a good time with them. [Reflection]

STUDENT: Yeah, mostly.

TEACHER: And sometimes they distract you or get you mad and you end up getting suspended. [Reflection]

STUDENT: Yeah, and then my mother gets mad at me.

TEACHER: That must not be fun either. So, tell me, how else was it like while you were away? [Open question]

STUDENT: Just boring being home with my grandmother all day. They wouldn't even let me play my video games.

TEACHER: That's three things you didn't like about staying home. You couldn't see your friends, your mother got upset with you, and it was pretty boring at home without your video games. [Summary]

STUDENT: I guess so.

TEACHER: Maybe we can come up with some ideas together about how you can have fun with your friends without getting in trouble? Tomorrow I have a little time after class so we can talk again, OK?

STUDENT: Sure.

The teacher and the student are reasonably well engaged, and the focus is clear. After class the next day they sit down for a few minutes.

TEACHER: We talked a bit already yesterday about what it was like being suspended. Tell me some more about how your behavior can be better?

STUDENT: Sometimes I get in trouble when I'm having fun, but it's not always me, it's my friends too. [Ambivalence]

TEACHER: Sometimes your friends do things also. You do seem to want to have fun without the trouble. [Reflection]

STUDENT: Yeah. [Change talk]

TEACHER: Let me ask you, how much do you want to stay out of trouble and keep doing that good work you showed me yesterday? [Open question to evoke change talk]

STUDENT: A lot, I guess, I don't like getting into trouble. [Change talk]

TEACHER: You want to try to make things different. [Reflection of change talk]

STUDENT: Well, I don't want to get suspended like that because it just gets worse and my mother gets upset with me. [Change talk] It's just hard to pay attention when I sit next to some of my friends . . . we mess around.

TEACHER: Could I give you a suggestion? [Seeking permission]

STUDENT: OK.

TEACHER: I wonder if we changed your seat, so you were closer to the front, it might help you stay out of trouble during work time. That way you could do more good work and still have fun time with your friends at lunch, recess, gym, and those places.

STUDENT: OK. Maybe. [Change talk]

TEACHER: You're a little unsure and you are still willing to give it a try. [Double-sided reflection] I appreciate that. Let's talk some more next week to see how things are going. Sound good?

STUDENT: Yup.

Commentary

Change can be fired in an instant or take years to unfold. This teacher has laid the foundation for further conversations, and few will doubt the likelihood of further struggles for this student. What's most evident in the above exchange is the emergence of the student's change talk, and the teacher's patient and supportive response to it. While the specifics of the dialogue would be different with an older student, the teacher would still put the student's own reasons for change front and center. That's the heart of MI.

Across Ages

For students even younger than the one we describe, the teacher would use a similar approach of relying on simple language, simple reflections, and capturing what the student identifies as important. For older students, teachers can use more complex reflections and discuss how the student sees his or her future *with and without change*.

Scenario 9.3. Preventing a Fight in the Hall

Scenario

A principal comes down the stairs into a crowded locker area and immediately notices: a small, growing circle, raised voices, and all eyes on two 16-year-old girls in the center. Maria flings her bag down at the legs of Leanne and shouts, "OK, Why!? Why did you do that!?" Leanne has allegedly posted unkind and untrue things about Maria on the Internet. The principal disperses the crowd and takes Maria to one side, starting a conversation about how she might want to consider options that she will not regret later.

What the Scenario Illustrates

How engagement can diffuse anger: MI can be useful in times of heightened emotion, to tame the situation, resolve conflict, and help a very angry and upset student consider new ways of tackling problems. By using the spirit and the core skills of MI—open questions, affirmation, reflecting, and summaries (OARS)—behavior can change. The goal here is a modest one, not to bring the two students together, but to illustrate using MI with one of them.

Setting Your Sights

This principal starts with a broad goal, not just to break up the conflict, but also to help Maria learn to handle things better, and conform to school rules. Being publicly insulted on the Internet has clearly threatened her self-image. MI can help the principal in a number of ways. Use of affirmation can lessen defensiveness and highlight Maria's strengths. Reflective listening can ensure that she feels understood and more likely to respond positively. Questions like "How might you handle this in a way that you won't regret later?" can help her to turn the corner and consider change. Her answers will include change talk.

It's usually best to engage first, which means listening carefully to how Maria feels and summarizing this for her, to demonstrate that you understand her.

Traps to Avoid

Focusing on who is to blame: Looking for the culprit can be risky to begin with. Knowing that it often takes two to start a fight, it's probably not wise for this principal to make premature assumptions about blame. The immediate goals are to stop a fight from happening and to prevent future trouble. Blaming and punishment are not necessarily the best or the only ways to proceed. For example, it will not help to walk in saying things like, "Right, what's going on here!?" and then focusing on getting the students to accept responsibility for what happened. This will likely generate defensiveness, with each party blaming the other. They could walk away seething with resentment and likely to repeat their behavior at another time. MI offers an opportunity to approach conflict resolution in a different way, compatible with what is sometimes called a restorative approach to resolving conflict. In this scenario this is realized through an informal relationship-building conversation that avoids punishment or discipline in the first instance.

In Practice

The principal approaches the conflict zone, and uses a directing style to disperse the crowd.

PRINCIPAL: OK, we are going to break this up now, so please step aside *(firm yet calm)*. OK *(to the crowd)*, please go to your classes. We won't be solving this right now (*taking a tearful Maria to one side, away from the crowd*).

PRINCIPAL: Let's talk for a minute. You seem pretty upset. What's up?

STUDENT: Nothing. I'm good (*straightening her clothes, clearly very angry*).

PRINCIPAL: I can get you a pass for your next class if you're willing to take a few minutes to talk. [Supporting her autonomy]

STUDENT: It's Leanne who needs talk!

PRINCIPAL: I noticed that you said something to Leanne that seemed like you were very angry with her. I haven't seen you upset like that before. It's not like you to be quick tempered. [An affirmation about how she normally deals with anger]

STUDENT: No, but I'm dealing with Leanne, who I thought was a friend. (*Looks up for the first time.*) Leanne is a hypocrite and she's posting things about me that are not true. I need to show her that she can't mess with me.

PRINCIPAL: You're very upset about it and you feel the need to stop it once and for all. [Reflection that enhances engagement]

STUDENT: Yes, by kicking her ass. She better stop posting lies about me. I'm not putting up with it any more.

PRINCIPAL: Leanne's posted something that's not true and you're worried other students might believe it. [Reflection that acknowledges her real concern and enhances engagement]

STUDENT: Yeah, they don't all know me that well, so they might. I hate her. When I walk down the hall, I feel like everyone is staring at me. (*She's starting to calm down and engage more in the conversation.*) I didn't even want to come to school today. [Yet she *did* come to school, so the principal assumes that school is in some way important to her.]

PRINCIPAL: You want to get back at her for what she did, and at the same time you decided to come to school today, so I imagine that you might want to resolve this without it affecting your status in school. [Reflection: a guess; points Maria in a positive direction]

STUDENT: Well, if I beat her up, I'd get suspended and get behind, plus my parents will get involved. [Change talk] She can't be doing this though!

PRINCIPAL: So, you'd like to figure out how to clear your reputation and avoid getting into trouble. [Reflection in response to change talk]

STUDENT: I guess that's right, yeah, I need this cleared up so I can get on with my life. [Change talk]

PRINCIPAL: What could you do?

STUDENT: I'd like to be able to teach her a lesson, but the most important thing is that she stop posting things about me. She's just jealous.

PRINCIPAL: She's doing it because she thinks she's competing with you [Reflection] and you have the insight to realize what is going on. [Affirmation] Ultimately you are looking for ways to get her to stop. [Reflection]

STUDENT: (*She takes a deep breath and pauses before answering.*) I don't know, someone just needs to tell her to stop. If I'm in a room with her though I'm not sure I could hold myself back.

PRINCIPAL: If you do sit down with her you'll need some help and to wait a little bit to settle down. [Reflection]

STUDENT: I guess if you can help arrange for us to talk it might get her to stop. [Change talk]

PRINCIPAL: The fact that you decided to work with everyone to resolve this without fighting shows a lot about your character, despite the resentment you have toward what she did. [Affirmation] Let me get back to you about arranging the talk with Leanne. OK? Let me get your pass.

STUDENT: All right.

Commentary

Two things happened in this exchange. First, the principal was able to diffuse anger by using mostly reflection. In this sense, MI skills are ideally suited to helping angry and upset students to calm down. It's what you might call a restorative conversation. Then a second process unfolded, evoking, where they worked together to find a solution, relying as much as possible on the student's own motivation and ideas.

Schools will vary in how they might bring the two students together, for example, by using a counselor, dean, administrator, mediator, talking circles, or a peace room. Illustrated here is a simple outcome of using MI: instead of proposing, suggesting, or enforcing a solution on a student like Maria, the principal gave her 5 minutes of time, came alongside her [engagement], and then elicited the solution from her. It might not always work out that easily, but in this case it is likely this conflict will not turn into a fight. Ideally, the student will feel respected, less distressed by the situation, and able to be more engaged in her education. Hopefully, this will be a learning experience about being able to tackle situations like this in the future.

Few individuals regardless of age are prepared to problem-solve at times of heightened emotion, so relying on engagement initially is important. *Acceptance,* an aspect of the MI spirit, can be particularly useful here; it allowed the principal to acknowledge the difficulty the student faced without necessarily condoning her behavior. For younger students, the conversation may eventually focus on choices that can be evoked from the students themselves and the more immediate benefits or consequences of those choices.

Learning

The facilitation of significant learning rests
on certain attitudinal qualities that exist
in the personal relationship between the
facilitator and the learner[s].
                                        —*Carl Rogers*

The previous chapter illustrated how MI might help with behavior problems, particularly social behavior problems. This one turns to its use for promoting learning. It's about academic behavior, efforts by students to learn, grow, and change. We don't see social and academic behaviors as separate topics or problem areas, requiring different approaches to motivation. For both types of behavior, it's all but impossible to insert learning and change into students. They have choices about how much to engage and change and, not surprisingly, their motivation to learn is variable and not always predictable. Conversation, an unsung virtue of artful teaching, is one of the main channels through which efforts can be made to engage and motivate students. Get this side of teaching right, better relationships, and other things like grades, attendance, and disruptive behavior, are easier for all involved.

The aim of this chapter is to unpack what helpful conversation informed by MI looks and feels like in and around the classroom. At the

*Social and academic
behaviors are not separate
problem areas, requiring
different approaches.*

center of this effort is enhancing motivation to learn. The scenarios below cover the use of MI with a whole class and with an individual student.

The Contribution of MI

MI can help promote learning for these reasons:

1. MI is keenly focused on enhancing internal motivation to change. Learning is a type of change, which involves a confluence of intentions and actions.
2. Skills like reflective listening and skillful informing can be easily integrated into subject-matter teaching.
3. Small moments matter. Short conversations, even a single question or brief acknowledgment of freedom of choice, can turn things around for students. MI is a guide to getting the most out of these everyday teaching moments.

Scenario 10.1. "I Just Don't Get It!"

Scenario

Both the teacher and the 15-year-old student know that the student is struggling with math. They have a short one-on-one conversation while the rest of the class is working in groups. How can her motivation to improve be enhanced? Is this due to a lack of effort or a lack of confidence in being able to understand the material?

What the Scenario Illustrates

The evoking process in an everyday teaching practice: Evoking solutions and change talk can be aided by exchanging ideas using the elicit–provide–elicit strategy (see Chapter 8) and by using the ruler (see Chapter 6) to assess math anxiety. Fear about learning can create ambivalence and self-doubt. MI-informed conversation can help to normalize the experience and facilitate change.

Setting Your Sights

Encouraging students gives them courage. Guiding that elicits change talk can be useful with those who lack confidence. You rely on students'

ability to solve problems by searching with them for solutions. The use
of affirmation, for example, can
provide a key to helping them over
a hurdle.

> *Guiding that elicits change talk can help students who lack confidence.*

Traps to Avoid

The righting reflex: Telling a student what to do can backfire. Being given all the answers can depress the courage to learn. Engagement will be undermined. Your conversation skills can instead help to draw out solutions from the student. If you provide suggestions, you can do this by offering choices (see Chapter 8).

The belief that the ability to learn is fixed, or innate, is often the result of experiencing repeated failure. When students doubt their ability to learn or do something, conversations can either increase or decrease their sense of confidence.

In Practice

The teacher approaches the student in the class, while other students are busy.

TEACHER: I've noticed that you seem a bit uncertain about what we are doing.

STUDENT: I hate math, I am no good at it. [Sustain talk]

TEACHER: Sometimes you feel like you just want to give up on math. [Reflection, paying attention to nonverbal cues]

STUDENT: Yup, if I could, I would.

TEACHER: It's not your favorite class. [Smiling; engagement is growing]

STUDENT: It's too hard, I don't get it! I've always had trouble with math. I don't think I'll ever understand this stuff. [Sustain talk]

TEACHER: Despite that, you've stuck with it and are willing to talk about it. [affirmation] I'll be right back, and when I do, how about this; you tell me about a situation when you did not know how to do something and then you figured it out? [Open question aimed at building self-efficacy; the start of evoking]

When the teacher returns, they have a conversation about the student's difficulty understanding how her new phone worked; it required reading the manual and also getting help from friends.

TEACHER: You started frustrated with the phone and then you worked it out. [Affirmation]

STUDENT: I depend on my phone for everything.

TEACHER: Now you couldn't do without it. [Reflection] What similarity might there be with math? [Open question: an adaption of the elicit–provide–elicit strategy: this is the first phase: understanding the student's needs and concerns before providing ideas that might help]

STUDENT: Well, I mean, it's not like I'll be able to use it. [Sustain talk]

TEACHER: You don't see the value at this point, yet you want to pass the class. [A guess about underlying ambivalence using a double-sided reflection]

STUDENT: Yes, that's true, I need the credits and don't want to go to night or summer school to make up credits. [Change talk]

TEACHER: I wonder what will be helpful to you now?

STUDENT: I'm not sure how I'm going to understand it. [Sustain talk] I can see I need help. [Change talk]

TEACHER: You'd like to get some kind of assistance. [Reflection]

STUDENT: If I could. [Change talk]

TEACHER: Can I make some suggestions? [The "provide" phase of the elicit–provide–elicit strategy]

STUDENT: Sure.

TEACHER: Tell me what makes the most sense to you: I'm here to explain things if you want; there's the tutor in the library after school; I could give you some links to learning online at home; and there's other students who you could ask for help from. What do you think about any of these options? [The final— "elicit"—phase of the elicit–provide–elicit strategy]

STUDENT: Well, some of them sound OK. But, I don't like asking questions in class. I'd like to be in a different small group, one where I'd feel more comfortable asking questions. [Change talk]

The teacher responds to this change talk by agreeing to set up this arrangement, then decides to evoke commitment talk by using a "ruler."

TEACHER: On a scale of 1 to 10, how committed are you to working in this smaller group?

STUDENT: Maybe a 5.

TEACHER: Can I ask you why a 5 and not a 2 or 3? [Asking why not something lower can be a useful way to evoke change talk]

STUDENT: Because, I guess I need to do better. I need to pass. [Change talk] I'm just not sure I can. Maybe tutoring will help too. [More change talk]

TEACHER: So, like asking your friends about the phone, you're thinking of going to tutoring in the library, and you've agreed that if I change you to a small group you will be more open to asking questions. [Summary]

STUDENT: Yes, that's right.

TEACHER: Let's touch base after school next Friday. Maybe you can tell me how things are going. [This may be all it takes to get the student to take the steps to do what it takes to get on track, or more conversations will be needed.]

Commentary

This scenario illustrates how the spirit and skills of MI can be brought to bear on everyday teaching. It entails a simple shift from telling to eliciting. The teacher moved through the four processes (see Chapter 4) by engaging briefly to begin with. The focus was obvious and provided by the student. Evoking required patience, along with a belief, conveyed to the student, that she can and does solve difficult problems in everyday life. The student expressed her ambivalence about math; the teacher acknowledged this and responded particularly to the change talk. Planning involved presenting a choice of possible solutions, and the student chose the one that made sense to her. Then the teacher returned to evoking to build her commitment, knowing that the more the student hears herself say why and how she might change, the more likely she is to change.

> *The more the student hears herself say why and how she might change, the more likely she is to change.*

Across Ages

Students of any age are likely to respond to affirmations and encouragement. To persist with a math assignment, a younger student may need a past math success to help bolster motivation or have the assignment broken down so as to start from a foundation of success.

Scenario 10.2. Students Never Come to Class Prepared

Scenario

An English teacher of high school juniors is frustrated because most of her students do not do their reading assignments at home. Explaining, persuading, and lecturing them about the consequences of this do not seem to make things better. This year she makes a decision to try an MI-informed conversation with one of her classes.

What the Scenario Illustrates

The "elicit–provide–elicit" strategy for giving information; using reflection to limit discord in the classroom: Two contrasting conversations are used below to highlight how to motivate students to do their reading assignments. In both cases the teacher seeks to engage students in a discussion; however, in the second one, there is an attempt to use their internal motivation, framed by the elicit–provide–elicit strategy described in Chapter 8. The teacher also uses reflections and affirmations to limit the potential discord or a collective resistance to the assignment. Parts of the conversation are abbreviated to avoid repetition for ease of comparison.

Setting Your Sights

It's easy to feel at a loss when there is pressure to cover material and students aren't doing their part. Instead of emphasizing rewards and punishments, the teacher intends to meet students' need for autonomy by nurturing their curiosity and internal motivation to learn. The teacher needs to hear many excuses for the inability to do the work [sustain talk], while at the same time focusing on change talk. Providing information about the assignment thoughtfully using the elicit–provide–elicit strategy can make a difference by taking the controlling sting out of the task at hand.

Traps to Avoid

Undermining autonomy: The teacher needs to avoid eliciting students' feelings of being controlled, which can squelch innate curiosity and interest. Just like pushing an individual to change, trying to push the group to read or learn can elicit a similar response. Trying to entice students with rewards can also be perceived as controlling and the rewards offered usually seem inad-

> *Promote learning as a dance rather than as a wrestling match.*

equate. It's best to promote learning and rigor as an enjoyable dance rather than a wrestling match. Students will dance because they like it, not because of any prize.

In Practice

This conversation is with 16- to 17-year-old students in an English class about the next assignment. Students are asked to select and read one of two books over the next month. Prior experience suggests that only a fraction will complete the assignment and those who begin it often quit. Here are two conversations: the first is the teacher's usual approach; the second one is MI-consistent.

Conversation A

TEACHER: Before I explain your next reading assignment, I'd like to tell you that I picked two books that I know you will like, so there should be no excuses about the reading being boring. I'd also like to say that you must keep up with the reading or your grade will suffer. We'll have a pizza party in the end if everyone does the reading. Here they are. As you can see, they are not the same size, and you'll pick which one, either the novel or short stories. Are you ready to get into some fun reading?

STUDENTS: (*Blank looks, no reply.*)

TEACHER: Anyhow, they are both about young people your age that don't have it easy. I won't give away any of the stories, but they need courage and determination. Sound familiar? They can be serious and funny at the same time. I know you'll like either one! For some of you, it might be the first book you will read from front to back. I'll be proud of you, especially if you pick the 336-page book rather than 160-page one. You will have quizzes, reports, and discussion about these books over the next 4 weeks. The highest grade you can get reading the shorter book is a B. Is that clear? Any questions?

STUDENT 1: What if when you read you can't get your mind to

focus for more than a few minutes? That's too many pages a week; that's unreal! [Sustain talk]

STUDENT 2: There is no way, that's way too much reading! [Sustain talk]

TEACHER: I want to remind you that your grade will suffer if you don't keep up; I'm giving you choices. You'll just have to pick. You can go for the shorter one. If you want the pizza party, you'll all have to keep up [Persuasion using the righting reflex].

STUDENT 3: What if we don't have time? Its football season and our coaches have us doing hours of practice after school. [Sustain talk]

STUDENT 4: I work after school and don't have that much time. [Sustain talk]

TEACHER: Come on, you know well that you make time for what you want. In high school, we don't hold your hand like your elementary teachers did. So, you'll just have to get serious, especially if you want to go to college. Getting good at reading will be valuable all your lives. Believe me, you'll like reading these! [Persuasion]

STUDENT 5: You don't get it; we have assignments and reports in all our classes. This is too much! [Sustain talk]

TEACHER: I'm sure you all want to pass this class, and this is a big part of your grade. If you keep up with the reading, the quizzes, reports on chapters, and discussions will be easy, and that will determine your grade.

STUDENT 6: What will it take to just pass this class? I'm OK with a D.

TEACHER: I do hope you all want to do more than the minimum. You all have so much potential. So, that is your next reading assignment. Please write down your choice of which book and turn it in on the way out.

Conversation B

TEACHER: Before I explain your next reading assignment, I'd like to ask you to jot down your thoughts about what you like about reading. [The "elicit" phase of the elicit–provide–elicit strategy]

STUDENT 1: I don't. It's boring. [Sustain talk]

TEACHER: Just be honest, about reading in general. Maybe you are curious about something. If you can't think of anything positive, you can jot down what you don't like about reading instead. Let's go for a few minutes. (*Time . . .*) OK. What have you come up with? [Open question]

STUDENT 2: I sometimes like reading what my friends post. [Change talk]

STUDENT 3: That stuff is so lame. It always the same people, writing blah-blah. [Sustain talk]

TEACHER: So people have different preferences regarding reading. [Reflection]

STUDENT 4: I enjoy following certain people, not my friends, I mean famous ones. [Change talk]

STUDENT 3: Sounds boring [Sustain talk]

STUDENT 5: I like reading stories. It's like a movie in my mind. [Change talk]

TEACHER: Reading can take you places in your mind, like to a different reality. [Reflection]

STUDENT 5: Yes, it's like you're there in other places. Like you are a different person. [Change talk]

TEACHER: Just by reading! Reading for some of you allows for vivid imaginations. [Affirmation] You allow your mind to take you into the story or follow people. [Reflection]

STUDENT 6: I like reading Internet searches to learn about stuff that I'm interested in. [Change talk]

TEACHER: And you dig deeper by reading. [Reflection] How are Internet searches helpful to the rest of you? [Open question]

STUDENT 7: When you have to write papers or find out about how to do something, making it easier to learn about things.

TEACHER: All by reading, it helps you pass your classes or learn about things you enjoy. [Reflection] Here's an idea about reading [The "provide" phase of the elicit–provide–elicit strategy] If you enjoy reading about celebrities, and other things, and you do this quite a lot, it pays off in grades now, in college, and in life. Like other things, it gets easier with practice. So, if you aren't much of a reader, might you want to challenge yourself to read?

STUDENT 8: If it's interesting, maybe. [Change talk]

TEACHER: So that brings us to the next assignment. [The "provide" phase of the "elicit–provide–elicit strategy] You get to pick one of two books, a novel or a book of short stories. They both are about young people your age. [Teacher talks about the books, their length, the planned group-work learning, reports, and grading.] OK, so what does this mean for you and your choice of book? [The third "elicit" phase of the "elicit–provide–elicit strategy]

STUDENT 9: It takes me too long to read even one chapter. I've got football practice and lots of things to do after that. [Sustain talk]

TEACHER: Your time is important to you and you only want to do things that are interesting or valuable to you. You like practicing football, and you've gotten good at it. [Reflection] With reading, it's up to you. [Emphasizing autonomy]

STUDENT 10: I work after school and finding time to read a lot is not going to be easy. [Sustain talk]

STUDENT 2: Maybe it's like reading posts, I could do it bit by bit. [Change talk]

TEACHER: So everyone has choices and decisions to make. Please write down your choice and why and turn it in on the way out. Of course, your effort will help determine your grade.

Commentary

Both conversations A and B present the next assignment with the goal of hooking the students. Notice the level of engagement in each. In B, students were asked to write and share what they liked about reading and so they did more than complaining; it took a bit longer but this will likely save time later.

Autonomy, a key part of the spirit of MI, was embedded in the way the conversation unfolded. Evoking students' ideas and opinions and reflecting them back honored students' autonomy. The teacher didn't leave it there. She reminded students that doing the assignment was their choice.

Across Ages

In conversations with a whole class, regardless of age, attempts to get students interested in learning assignments can be helped by providing students with choices. Conversations that acknowledge students' opinions (reflections), that provide positive feedback (affirmations), that offer an explanation for any requirements or behavior restrictions, and that reflect back student emotional reactions, will increase their willingness, engagement, and hopefully their interest. You will find this is particularly helpful with students seeking more independence, like most adolescents.

Scenario 10.3. "You're All Facing Change: Let's Discuss This"

Scenario

A class of 14-year-olds is facing change, a move to a new school. A teacher decides to help them anticipate the change, including how they might handle strong emotion like getting angry in the face of hormonal and other changes. Rather than give a lecture, the teacher attempts to evoke students' thoughts, feelings, and imagination so they can be better prepared for change.

What the Scenario Illustrates

The spirit and skills of MI in a classwide discussion: MI's spirit and skills are used to provide new information and discuss the implications of change. This type of conversation can be had with any age group.

Note

We are aware that teacher training on how to conduct classwide discussion is usually minimal. Our hope here is to champion this activity and show how the skills of MI can augment and improve current practice.

Setting Your Sights

Skills like reflection and affirmation can be used in most classwide discussions. Perhaps none are more useful than when looking to the future, something that is both worrying and exciting to students. Ambivalence will be a common theme. The teacher here will be looking first to engage the students, and when a focus on change is established, to evoke their ideas about tackling the challenges to come.

Traps to Avoid

Too much directing: Lecturing and speeches have their place, for example, covering material quickly or preparing students for tests. However, it's difficult to retain interest and motivation if students are not involved in actively exploring and sharing ideas and solutions.

In Practice

The teacher starts by asking the class a question.

> TEACHER: Now that you are finishing this year, what do you think will be different in your next school? [Open question]
>
> STUDENT 1: I think we'll have harder homework and classwork.
>
> STUDENT 2: My cousin says that in some of his classes he does more work with others in groups.
>
> STUDENT 3: I think we'll have more chances to be with our friends.
>
> TEACHER: So, on the one hand you anticipate that things will be harder and on the other hand some of you are looking forward to more time with friends [Reflection, double-sided].
>
> STUDENT 4: I heard that we'll have lots of teachers, instead of just one and that some of them do fun things. I'm not saying we don't like just having you. Isn't that right?
>
> TEACHER: You're right, you'll move from class to class for your different subjects. You're uncertain how that is going to be for you. [Reflection]
>
> STUDENT 5: I heard there is something called Advisory, like a short class that we have with one of our teachers.
>
> STUDENT 6: My older sister said it's a class you hear about school things and talk about different issues, but there are no grades and it meets for less time.
>
> TEACHER: You guys know so much already, maybe there is no need to talk about it! [Affirmation]
>
> STUDENT 7: I hear that they give students only 4 minutes to get from one class to another, which I hear is a pain if you have to go to the bathroom.
>
> TEACHER: So, you've described how some things will be structured differently with a new school than they are now. You'll likely have to stay on top of your assignments, class work will sometimes involve groups, and you'll be moving from one class to another; with a group of other classmates you'll be assigned to a homeroom and a homeroom teacher for announcements and important discussion. You recognize that these are big changes

regarding school. [Summary; engagement is reasonably established] Can I ask you what other changes you think you have coming, now that you are entering adolescence? Like changes that happen in your brain? [The teacher provides the focus]

STUDENTS: (*Period of silence*)

STUDENT 2: I heard that hormones cause changes in our bodies. I don't know about my brain.

STUDENTS: (*Some laughter*)

TEACHER: Are you interested in hearing about what happens in your brains during the next few years?

STUDENTS: (*Attentiveness, a few reply*) Sure; OK.

TEACHER: This is a time when huge changes begin to go on in your brain, and as you mentioned, hormones have a lot to do with it. Connections in the brain that you don't use get pruned away, while others get stronger. Anyone want to describe things you've noticed? [Open question]

STUDENT 8: What does pruned mean?

TEACHER: Cut or trimmed away, disconnected.

STUDENT 5: It seems like I get more moody sometimes and I get bored with some things I used to like.

STUDENT 9: I like to hang out with more people than I used to, including boys.

STUDENTS: (*Laughter*)

STUDENT 2: Jeremy, she's talking about you! (*Laughter*)

TEACHER: OK, so you notice that your emotions are stronger [Reflection] and there is an explanation for that: your hormones cause changes, one of which is it make your emotions more powerful; so feelings like love or even anger are stronger and that of course influences your behavior. How might that affect you in school? [Provides more focus]

STUDENT 10: It won't. I haven't noticed anything different and I can control myself.

STUDENT 9: Well, adults are on my case more than they used to be and I'll admit it makes me mad, but I think that's just me, I've been that way a long time. (*Silence*)

TEACHER: Anyone else? How might having stronger emotions affect you in school next year? [Open question]

STUDENT 2: I guess maybe people will get into more fights.

STUDENT 7: Like people will get jealous and get into hassles.

STUDENT 9: You might fall in love.

TEACHER: So your thoughts and feelings can affect your behavior and that might mean the possibility of fights or feeling really close to another person. You know what happens when you get in fights in school. How might you deal with these strong emotions that could hijack your brain away from learning? [Open question]

STUDENT 11: Like, try to keep in control. [Change talk]

STUDENT 2: Ignore people that bother you. [Change talk]

STUDENT 7: Look who's talking.

TEACHER: And practice makes perfect, right? Can I mention something that studies show about how to deal with strong emotions like anger? [Provides more focus]

STUDENTS: (*Curious and attentive, a nonverbal yes.*)

TEACHER: They notice that if you tell yourself the emotion you are feeling, like "I'm getting mad," that it can help you keep from having your brain hijacked. That is the work of the prefrontal cortex (*touching forehead*), which is the last part of our brains to fully develop; it is where you plan, decide what is right and wrong, and control yourself. So, let's pretend you are starting to get mad and you just told yourself "I'm getting mad." I'd like to go around the room and ask you to say something positive you could do next to keep from going off. Think for a minute, be creative; what would help you change your mood? If you're not ready to decide, you can say "pass." I would imagine that you all have things you enjoy doing or thinking about that could help refocus your mind. Who wants to start?

STUDENT 2: I'll go; I could listen to music! [Change talk]

TEACHER: Let's just continue around, but you can take your time to think, OK?

STUDENT 9: I'd go throw some hoops, or if I couldn't do that then at least think about playing basketball soon. [Change talk]

STUDENT 12: I'd play a game on my tablet. [Change talk]

STUDENT 13: And I'd play video games. [Change talk]

STUDENT 14: I'd go for a walk . . . [Change talk]

TEACHER: Lots of creativity in this room. You each know yourself well and what might help you. [The discussion continues.]

Conversations in classes and schools will take place in different ways for sharing information, brainstorming, or maintaining order and structure. When we want change to happen, consider putting on your MI hat, and shift to this guiding conversational style. Educational transitions force changes on students that they are often not prepared for. MI can be ideal in helping students in a class setting prepare for those changes. But the methods could be used for a frank conversation about anything. Box 10.1 describes how MI can be woven into an exercise for students.

MI helps students prepare for educational transitions.

BOX 10.1. Learning to Change

MI can be woven into other tasks and exercises for students. It's the awareness of the importance of change talk that can lend additional weight to an activity. Here's an example of a small-group discussion in which I (R. R.) helped students in a school in Chicago to address a problem, for example, handling feelings of anger. They discussed the challenges, and as a last exercise we conducted a "memory circle challenge" as follows: The first student came up with the best idea he could think of for handling his feelings of anger; it quite naturally took the form of change talk ("I am going to walk away from the situation"); then the next student had to remember and repeat what the first one came up with, and produce his own change talk; the third student had to remember both of them, and produce her own, and so on right around the circle. What they heard was repetitions of their own and others' change talk.

11

Personal Growth

During these [MI] sessions the boundaries
of gangs, hate, low self-esteem, and poverty
seem to disappear, and if only for a moment,
the students have an opportunity to become
kids and learn.
—*Crystal Winifeld Edwards,*
school social worker

Some conversations with students are not about "school" per se, but about life, friends, or the future. They might fall outside of one's standard job description, but they are common, and children need them if they are to thrive. We aren't suggesting you become a student's personal counselor. However, MI can be used to improve your relationships and conduct these more personal conversations, whether formal or informal, very brief or more prolonged. The three scenarios in this chapter focus on issues that impact school experience.

The first scenario is a conversation between a teacher and student about a social problem. The second scenario has a stronger educational feel, about decisions early in the school year about how much energy the student might invest in his studies. The third scenario is a discussion between an administrator and a student who was recently arrested.

Some of the conversations students need to have with you are not about school.

The Contribution of MI

Here are some reasons why MI might help with students' personal growth:

1. Personal challenges affect learning, counseling services are often not readily available, and teachers on the front line often know the students better than anyone else. MI provides a way to be helpful, in even brief conversations, because it is forward-looking, and allows students to clarify what they really want.
2. Making choices and learning how to problem-solve is how students grow. This cuts across academic and personal matters, and they influence each other.
3. MI is founded on engagement, a platform for sharing ideas between teachers and students.

Scenario 11.1. "I'm So Torn!"

Scenario

A 17-year-old girl stops by her social studies teacher's class after school to discuss a dilemma she is facing. She needs to decide whether to maintain contact with a peer group that is engaging in behavior that makes the student uncomfortable or limiting her contact at the risk of losing friendships.

What the Scenario Illustrates

Using core skills to evoke change: The teacher explores ambivalence by staying curious, focusing on what a student really values, and trusting that a solution can be evoked from her. It's possible to express concerns, as needed, by asking permission.

Setting Your Sights

A student feels very ambivalent; there are clear choices and she is confused and upset. She will express her conflicting motivations in the form of change talk and sustain talk. The teacher needs to be ready for it to sound confused and full of contradiction. MI involves hearing and reflecting these voices, and responding particularly to change talk aligned with the student's values, what she really wants. Restraint is important for giving the student space to resolve the ambivalence.

Traps to Avoid

Premature focus: Being too concrete and solution-focused is a trap that is easy to fall into when a student feels ambivalent. "So what are you going to do?" is often a question that mistakenly feels essential to ask, and soon. The discussion would then focus too narrowly on this specific issue and miss an opportunity for something broader and more fundamental. It might be captured in the question like, "What is most important to you right now?" A conversation that uses the specific issue as a platform to also consider and clarify a student's values may have benefits beyond the dilemma at hand. It often feels natural to use the "righting reflex," based on your genuine care for the student's welfare. However, when the "righting reflex" meets ambivalence, the student will voice only sustain talk and an unhelpful conversation often follows.

In Practice

The student walks into the classroom shortly after the last bell rings for the day.

> STUDENT: Mrs. _____, do you have a minute?
>
> TEACHER: Sure. Have a seat. What's up?
>
> STUDENT: Well, remember when we talked about my friend last week? The one I was worried about? [Student provides the focus, teacher remembers to engage first]
>
> TEACHER: Yes, of course. You said she's stopped caring about school. That she's mostly interested in going to parties and hanging out.
>
> STUDENT: Exactly. Well, she asked me if I wanted to go to a party this weekend with some of our other friends. And when I said I was busy she told me to "stop being so lame."
>
> TEACHER: You're starting to feel some pressure. [Reflection]
>
> STUDENT: Totally. I wasn't sure what to say after that so I kind of said maybe.
>
> TEACHER: You're feeling pretty stuck. [Reflection]
>
> STUDENT: Well, and now it's not just her. A few of our other friends are starting to hang out a lot at this guy's house and I'm just not really comfortable with it.
>
> TEACHER: What concerns you about all this? [Curious open

question. Engaging merges into evoking as ambivalence appears]

STUDENT: I don't know, I mean she was like my best friend for years. And even though we met new people in high school we were still really close. We did everything together, including our homework. Now it just seems like all she cares about is having fun and she expects me to join her all the time and I'm just like "Wait, what about school?!" It's not like I don't want to hang out with friends because I do. It's just that I don't want to start falling behind and I'm not sure I want to be around all that stuff at parties. I'm so torn!

TEACHER: You have a real dilemma here. Part of you wants to hang out and have fun and at the same time you are worried that she is going overboard with it. That she's stopped caring about school. [Double-sided reflection, avoiding the righting reflex and allowing her to share her wisdom]

STUDENT: Oh, I know she's going overboard. She basically told me that.

TEACHER: And so in some ways you are feeling that you have to choose between a good friend and school. Not to mention your concern about what kinds of things are going on at the parties. [Reflection that highlights the key element of ambivalence]

STUDENT: (*Puts head down.*) I just don't know what to do.

TEACHER: This involves some things that are really important to you. Like being a good friend, being a good student, and taking care of yourself. [Reflection that acts both as an affirmation and a statement highlighting some of her values]

STUDENT: Why do I have to choose anyway? Why can't she just respect that I'm not interested in going to that guy's house?

TEACHER: You seem pretty clear about what's important to you. [Reflection]

STUDENT: Well, as far as going to that guy's house and partying and stuff, I'm definitely saying no to that [Change talk]. I just know she's going to get mad at me.

TEACHER: Can I ask you a question? [Asking permission]

STUDENT: Sure.

TEACHER: What would it be like to talk with her about this? Not so much the decision for this weekend, more so about your friendship and the concerns you've been having. [Evoking her ideas]

STUDENT: I've thought about that. I tried texting her about it once but it was late and her mom made her put away her phone. I should probably try again though.

TEACHER: How do you think you will approach the conversation? [Another open question evoking her ideas]

STUDENT: I just need to be clear with her that I respect what she wants to do but that I still want to focus on school and don't really want to get into all that partying she's doing. Especially at that guy's house. [Change talk]

TEACHER: So being clear about the things that really matter to you like you've mentioned already. School, friendship, and taking care of yourself. [Reflection]

STUDENT: Exactly.

Commentary

Besides the consistent use of reflections and open questions, the teacher chose to highlight certain values apparent in the student's story. In doing so the teacher didn't voice an opinion per se. In fact, this is likely why the student felt comfortable approaching this teacher in the first place. The teacher's caring, nonjudgmental stance allowed the student to clarify for herself what was important in making this decision and in making a plan for the future.

This conversation could have gone in several directions. You may wonder how different it would have sounded had the student seemed more inclined to go to the party or expressed a waning interest in her schoolwork. Certainly the content of the dialogue would have changed, however, reflecting the student's values would still be important in guiding her decisions.

Across Ages

Although the importance of friendships seems to increase as students get older, friends are important to younger students too. When using MI with young children, the conversations may sound like Scenario 9.2, with more immediate implications and challenges. For example, the teacher might evoke ideas from younger students about how to be a good friend. This can be balanced with feedback from adults.

Affirmation(s) about how the student is a good friend or caring person could also have lasting effects.

Scenario 11.2. "He's Got Potential, but . . . "

Scenario

A 15-year-old boy has thus far been unable to reach his potential. He struggles academically and socially. A teacher meets with him at the start of the school year.

What the Scenario Illustrates

Evoking change: This is the heart of MI. The dialogue below shows how a brief conversation fueled by acceptance and core skills like affirmation can help a student. A key is eliciting what the student really wants from school.

Setting Your Sights

The teacher's starting point is not to pass judgment, but to focus on the student's values, goals and strengths. The teacher will also want to explore the student's belief in his ability to succeed.

Traps to Avoid

The righting reflex: Giving solutions can result in a too narrow focus, perhaps just on a few subject grades. It's better to start and harness the student's goals and strengths. It might also be tempting to give the student reasons why he should believe in himself and why he can succeed. But in using MI, the conversation flows in a different way. MI involves *drawing out* rather than *putting in.* This way the teacher honors the fact that the student is the expert on himself. Supporting autonomy as mentioned throughout this book can be particularly powerful because students want to feel in charge of their own lives.

> MI *involves drawing out rather than putting in.*

In Practice

The teacher asks to speak with the student, and the initial part of the conversation involves engagement, listening to how the student's summer went. The scenario continues from there.

TEACHER: Well, it sounds like you had a pretty nice break and were even able to save up some money. You are really dedicated to things you set your mind to. How are you feeling about the school year? [Brief summary with an affirmation. Then an open question about the school year.]

STUDENT: I don't know, to be honest with you. I mean, I never really liked school much. I always just did it because I felt I had to. Then last year I had all that trouble with Ms. Johnson [science teacher] and I was just like "Forget this!"

TEACHER: I remember. The two of you really seemed to butt heads. And yet somehow you were able to make it through the year with some good grades. [Reflection and affirmation with an unspoken invitation for the student to consider how he was able to succeed]

STUDENT: I guess I wanted to show her I wasn't as bad as she thought I was.

TEACHER: There's that determination again. [Affirmation]

STUDENT: (*Smiles, shrugs shoulders.*) If you want to call it that. Most people just say that I'm stubborn.

TEACHER: (*Laughs.*) Well, I can see that too. So you remember your experience from last year and are still thinking about how much energy to invest this year. [Double-sided reflection, the second half of which is purposeful and deliberately forward-looking, an invitation to discuss what the student's thoughts are about the upcoming year.]

STUDENT: Yeah, I'm still thinking about it. I know school is going to get harder so I won't be able to just skate by. [Change talk] I don't have Ms. Johnson anymore so I don't have to worry about that. But I don't want to spend time on classes that aren't going to help me when I get older. [Sustain talk—he is feeling ambivalent]

TEACHER: If you're going to invest the time, you want to be sure it will pay off for you. [Reflection to evoke more change talk]

STUDENT: Exactly. And this summer it was great to work in my uncle's shop. I mean the money was good and all, but he really taught me a lot about working on engines. I actually enjoyed it.

TEACHER: I bet you did some great work. Maybe it was the first time you worked hard at something that fit closely with your interests. [Reflection]

STUDENT: Totally! So why do I need to bust my butt doing homework to keep my grades up when I can just keep working with my uncle doing something I like and make some money? [Sustain talk]

TEACHER: As you consider your choices you're wondering what's going to keep you focused on school. [This is a reflection with purpose, designed to point the discussion toward the goal of doing better in school. So far the student seems to be leaning away from school and toward his new work experience. The reflection is not intended to argue against work but to keep the student thinking about how to be successful with school. It also supports the student's autonomy by acknowledging his "choices."]

STUDENT: I guess I was surprised with how hard it got to keep up last year. I don't know if I can do it again. [Sustain talk]

TEACHER: I'm curious how you were able to do it last year? Besides showing Ms. Johnson you could. [Open question exploring past success]

STUDENT: I just took advantage of time in school to do my work. I knew that if I left stuff for home it wouldn't get done. Staying after with you those days helped too, not just with my math but with other classes.

TEACHER: You know yourself pretty well. You developed a strategy and stuck with it. [Affirmation]

STUDENT: Back to that determination thing I guess.

TEACHER: That and making a plan that allowed you to take advantage of your resources, like staying after with me. [Another purposeful reflection designed to pair the student's strengths with determination and planning]

STUDENT: (pauses, thinking) Maybe I can go to the shop right after school and do my work there before helping out my uncle? [Change talk]

TEACHER: Rather than having to choose between school and the shop maybe pairing the two will work for you. [Reflection]

STUDENT: I can talk with my uncle about it. I'm sure he won't mind. He does try to push me to keep up with school. [Change talk]

TEACHER: Somebody else in your corner. [Reflection]

Commentary

With adequate engagement established, the teacher was able to demonstrate acceptance and enhance the student's confidence in his abilities in several ways. First, the teacher's use of affirmation was selective and purposeful, and highlighted the student's strengths and ability to succeed. Second, the teacher did not argue in favor of school, but highlighted the choices facing him. And third, the teacher stayed away from inserting any of his own ideas or advice; he kept his sights on evoking the student's natural planning skills. If the teacher had ideas of his own there would have been ways of suggesting options in a MI-consistent way [see Chapter 8]. In this particular conversation there was no need to, although the potential for doing this might well arise in further dialogues with this boy.

Across Ages

The conversation in this scenario relies on abstract concepts such as values and confidence in one's abilities. For younger students, teachers can evoke simpler concepts using open questions such as "What do you like at school?" These can be launching points for considering ways to improve effort in the classroom.

Scenario 11.3. Just a Bump in the Road?

Scenario

An administrator hears that a 17-year-old male student was arrested over the weekend and asks to meet with him. Although initially suspicious, the student eventually settles into a conversation about going forward.

What the Scenario Illustrates

Partnership is an element of the MI spirit that we highlight in this scenario. The collaborative nature of MI assumes that two experts exist in a conversation about change. The administrator uses all three communication styles here and creates an environment that allows for the sharing of ideas and opinions.

Setting Your Sights

Many administrators or school heads embrace a style that relies on "tough love." MI offers a somewhat different way of engaging with students, particularly those that feel hard to reach. The administrator in this scenario does not view her role as requiring "toughness." Her task initially is to express curiosity and demonstrate acceptance, in an effort to develop a partnership, one in which there is less of a contrast between expert adult and misbehaving student. She initially uses a following style to minimize defensiveness. It's assumed that the student had a difficult experience, and that by genuinely withholding judgment about who he is or what he should have learned, the possibility for learning might be enhanced. One

> *MI offers a way of engaging with students who feel hard to reach.*

judgment is present: this young man is capable of succeeding despite any poor choices he might have made, or the rough background he might have come from.

Traps to Avoid

Blaming: The administrator could assign blame and ask the student to "accept responsibility" in order to "teach the student a lesson." Blaming, however, frequently depresses rather than elevates someone's motivation to change.

In Practice

The student is called to the office over the loudspeaker. The principal calls him into her office.

> PRINCIPAL: Thanks for seeing me today. Have a seat.
>
> STUDENT: (*nervous and somewhat suspicious*) OK. What's this about?
>
> PRINCIPAL: Well, I wanted to touch base with you about something Officer Rodgers told me this morning. He said that you were arrested over the weekend at a party. I guess there was fight or something and he said you were involved.
>
> STUDENT: (*still defensive*) Yeah, well I guess you know about it then.
>
> PRINCIPAL: You might be a bit suspicious of my intentions here, which I understand. I'm not looking to lecture you or get on your case about anything. When this sort of thing happens with our students I try to meet with them briefly, see if we can help them in anyway. I also need to be sure that nothing that

happens outside of school impacts what goes on with the rest of our students. Does that clear things up? [The administrator starts with a reflection to capture how the student feels, then uses a directing style to be clear about her intentions.]

STUDENT: (*more puzzled than defensive now*) I guess. I still don't know what you want to talk about.

PRINCIPAL: Fair enough. Well like I said, I heard the story from Officer Rodgers. I was hoping though that you could tell me what happened from your eyes. [Engaging is now the priority, and a following style is the most efficient route]

STUDENT: I was at this party with some of my friends. We were about to get in the car when these dudes stepped up to us saying how one of my boys was messing with some girl. They jumped him so we started to fight. We weren't going to let him get jumped like that.

PRINCIPAL: They approached you and you defended your friend. [Reflection emphasizing protection of his friend]

STUDENT: (*letting down his guard a bit*) Yeah, we were just leaving and they stepped up to us. After a few minutes the fight ended and we got in the car and left. A few minutes later we got pulled over and the cops were saying how they received a report of a fight and we fit the description or something. So they arrested us all for disorderly conduct. It was messed up.

PRINCIPAL: You don't think it was fair. Maybe you're wondering how the cops heard about the fight in the first place. [More reflections here using a following style. The administrator is purposefully trying to listen to the student's story with genuine curiosity, knowing full well that the student will likely become defensive again if he begins to feel judged.]

STUDENT: Exactly. We weren't looking to start anything. We were just there having a good time. Then all of a sudden we get jumped and now I have to deal with the cops. My mother had to get called down to the station and she's all on my case about it, saying I could go to juvenile detention, telling me I'm going to be just like my father. I don't need any of this. [Change talk]

PRINCIPAL: From a fun night out with some friends to a pile of stress and headaches. You seem pretty concerned about it all. [Reflecting the change talk]

STUDENT: Well, who needs this kind of thing? I don't. [Change talk]

PRINCIPAL: I wonder what's next for you? [The administrator makes a gentle shift to a guiding style, focusing on the future, hoping to see whether he can express a constructive way forward.]

STUDENT: [Student is increasingly more comfortable, sharing information about his background and family situation.] This just isn't me. I don't get in trouble or anything. I mean I'm not going to let one of my friends get jumped, but I'm not like some of these other kids doing stupid stuff. I already got my father and older brother in jail. My little brother doesn't need to see this happen to me. [Change talk]

PRINCIPAL: Being a good role model for him is important to you. [Another affirmation, this time about his concern for his brother.]

STUDENT: I just want things to be better for him, that's all.

PRINCIPAL: What are some other ways you try to make things better for him, besides trying to stay out of trouble? [Begins discussion about how the student will handle himself now starting from what's important to the student, his brother, as opposed to the administrator's agenda.]

STUDENT: I'm still in school for one. No one in my family has graduated before and I promised my mother I would be the first. I might not have the best grades in the world but I do OK.

PRINCIPAL: Your mother is pretty important to you too. I'm curious about something, how is it that you dedicated yourself to showing your brother a different way to grow up? Where did that come from? [Another *guiding* question about personal qualities the student possesses that have helped him to this point and will likely help with the current challenges he faces]

STUDENT: I don't know, I guess I just saw how my mother didn't give up on us through all the struggles she had to go through. She was going to do whatever she could to make sure me and my brother had what we needed.

PRINCIPAL: She's quite an inspiration. [Reflection]

STUDENT: I guess you could say that.

PRINCIPAL: So this arrest is quite a departure for you. You are someone who is dedicated to your family, in particular your brother for whom you want to show a better way and your mother whom you admire a great deal for the commitment she's made to you both. You have also responded to difficult times in your past, specifically with your father and older brother going to prison, with a stronger commitment to school. [Summary capturing some of the key strengths the administrator heard from the student]

STUDENT: Pretty much.

PRINCIPAL: Would it be OK with you if we talked a bit about things going forward, in light of the arrest? [Asking permission, maintaining *partnership,* and supporting student's autonomy]

STUDENT: Sure, I guess.

PRINCIPAL: First, Officer Rodgers will likely check in with you a bit over the next few weeks. Depending on how the legal process unfolds, like if they assign you a probation officer, he may be in contact with that person as well. [Here's a shift to *directing* as the principal explains the procedures they use at the school to monitor students with legal problems.]

STUDENT: *(more annoyed)* Great, so I'll even have cops on my case here at school.

PRINCIPAL: Well, hopefully you won't feel any extra pressure with this. It's just one way we monitor these situations. However, if you think he's making things more stressful here at school, don't hesitate to tell me and we can see what we can do to change that, OK?

STUDENT: Sure.

PRINCIPAL: I'm also interested in knowing what we can do to help you during these next few weeks to keep you on track with your school goals? [A return to a guiding style: evoking his ideas]

STUDENT: I'm not sure really. I've never been through this before, so I don't really know what to expect.

PRINCIPAL: True, hard to know what you'll have to deal with. What if I gave you an open invitation to check back in with me if you think of something that would be helpful to you? Also know that we have other resources in the school for you, people like our school counselors that I'm sure would be happy to touch base with you as you navigate what's to come. You can decide. How does that sound? [Provides student with some options but leaves it up to the student to decide]

STUDENT: That's fine. If I think I need some help I'll check in with someone. [Change talk] I just don't want people to start judging me. I mean, this is just a bump in the road for me you know. [Change talk]

PRINCIPAL: You are determined to not let this event derail you from your commitments to your family, and to yourself. [Reflection of change talk]

Commentary

The administrator in this scenario used reflections early to create an environment where the student felt heard not judged, supported rather than vilified. Certainly, there could be more details to this story, such as whether the student had a less innocent role in the altercation. The administrator chooses to focus instead on the student's resilience, strengths, and personal resources for dealing with difficult situations. Using the student's own goals as the starting point she develops a partnership with him, offering him resources he can choose to take advantage of if he thinks they can help him. However, the administrator is still open with the student about how the school will respond, in this case using the school resource officer as a contact person to monitor the legal situation.

The last scenario above is clearly more relevant for older students more likely to have trouble with police. But consider that the heart of this scenario is a collaborative conversation about a fresh start, and then one can see its application with younger students. Students of all ages can return to school following a break related to a difficult experience. All three communication styles would fit into such a conversation: (1) a *following style* to listen and engage; (2) a *guiding style* to draw out more about what the student wants to achieve; and (3) a *directing style* to clarify rules and expectations.

12

Working with Families

Parents defend themselves only when they feel
threatened. Our shared interest in their child's
well-being has been a great platform for using MI.
—*School Administrator*

The opportunity to talk with parents is often infrequent and short. Skillful use of time sits at the heart of efficient conversation. It may be tempting to bluntly plow right into the situation and problem-solve *for* parents. This can be like pushing a rope. Change is often better achieved by collaborative problem solving, building on the strengths of all involved. This sounds easy in theory. How MI might help in practice is the focus of the three scenarios in this chapter.

> *Change is often better achieved by building on the strengths of all involved.*

The first scenario is a phone call to a parent, which as usual is due to a problem. These calls can be fraught with strong emotions and can elicit a threat response in a parent feeling blamed or inadequate. Parents may punish the student, leading to growing resentment and little or no change, all depending on the discussion that took place. Helping students learn from mistakes or getting support when needed is important and sometimes requires parents' help. What the teacher *does not* say is as important as what she does. Approaching conversations from the standpoint of parent as expert, without judgment, makes for more effective and efficient conversations.

116

The second scenario deals with a discussion of a student's report, where finger pointing is an ever-present danger. The third scenario involves a more challenging situa-

> *Approach conversations from the standpoint of parent as expert, without judgment.*

tion: the parent is angry. Listening is important for helping to calm things down and make sure that the parent feels heard. Only then can things turn toward resolution.

For this third scenario, we ask you, our readers, to decide how to respond to angry statements from three different parents. Four possible responses are offered for each parent statement. Which ones are MI-adherent? After you've made your choices, compare them with our explanations.

The Contribution of MI

Here are three reasons why MI might be helpful in conversations with parents:

1. The skills involved can be used to rapidly diffuse the tension that so often runs high in conversations with parents.
2. MI creates an atmosphere of acceptance that can cross cultural and other barriers that so frequently hamper progress.
3. MI can model to parents a way to communicate with their child.

Scenario 12.1. Making a Short Telephone Conversation Count

Scenario

Jimmy is 9 years old, and seems to single-handedly determine how each day goes. He does well some days, and on others he draws his peers into distracting play and disagreement and the classroom falls apart. The teacher decides to make a very brief telephone call to his mother.

What the Scenario Illustrates

Engaging, focusing, and evoking in a brief conversation designed to avoid blaming, develop partnership, and identify shared strategies for helping this boy.

Setting Your Sights

There has been minimal contact with the mother before this call and it's difficult to judge how she will react. Time is tight. Engagement will be critical at the outset, and beyond. Focus will be important too—the conversation will at some point address the behavioral difficulties in school. Attention can then turn to evoking, relying as much as possible on the mother's ideas. A good platform for MI will be to view child and mother as having strengths, and to point these out, using affirmation. How is it possible to specify problems without unduly labeling or "pathologizing" the child? A feeling of working in partnership usually ensures this won't happen, as does use of the core skills of MI.

Traps to Avoid

Judging and failing to engage: The mother could feel blamed and criticized for her ability to raise her child; defensiveness, disagreement, and discord could be just around the corner. The teacher here will seek to harness the mother's motivation to support her child's education. Very often when difficulties arise in the classroom with a student, parents have experienced a similar challenge at home and have already tried to make changes.

In Practice

Jimmy's mother answers the phone.

MOTHER: Hello.

TEACHER: Hi, this is Ms. Jones, Jimmy's teacher. How are you today?

MOTHER: Fine, thank you. How are you?

TEACHER: Doing OK. I called hoping we could spend a few minutes talking about how Jimmy is doing. Would that work for you right now?

MOTHER: Sure, I have some time. Is he in trouble or something?

TEACHER: Well, not exactly. I'm not calling because of a specific incident or anything like that. I did want to check in with you about how he is doing in our classroom though. If it's OK I wonder if you could tell me how you think the year has been going so far? [Open question; teacher elicits mother's impressions first; engagement is the top priority]

MOTHER: I don't know, I mean he doesn't tell me too much. Some days he gets home and it seems like he's had a rough day. He'll say that so and so was mean to him or that you took away some points. Other days he seems fine, he comes home, does a little bit of homework and that's it.

TEACHER: So a mixture of good days and not-so-good days from what you can tell. [Reflection]

MOTHER: Pretty much. Is that what's happening?

TEACHER: I think Jimmy's reports to you are probably pretty accurate. While he may not be the most talkative boy, he seems to share with you some of what's going on.

MOTHER: Yeah, we've managed pretty well these past several years. I don't try to push him or anything, but I also try to stay on top of how he's doing.

TEACHER: We appreciate that this side, and your involvement is clearly helping. It also seems like you have a good system with homework. He's been pretty consistent with that so far this year. [Affirmation]

MOTHER: Oh definitely, he struggled quite a bit last year with school work so I decided I needed to give him more help. More support at home.

TEACHER: And the benefits of your efforts are there in school too. [Affirmation] Perhaps toward the end of this call we can talk about what you find works for him at home. I wanted to make sure we also discussed his behavior today as well. I wonder if that's OK with you? [Focusing: making a decision with mother about what to talk about, i.e., the direction of the conversation; making sure that the teacher's agenda is clearly stated]

MOTHER: Yes, absolutely. What's happening?

TEACHER: Well, like I said I think your description earlier fits pretty well. Jimmy has plenty of good days where he's engaged, does his work, and gets along with others. [Genuinely emphasizes Jimmy's strengths] And then there are other days, like today, where he really struggles when I ask him to start working or try to redirect him from talking with his classmates [Notice the difference between "he really struggles" and "he behaves badly."] I think for the most part he gets along with the other kids but there are times when he seems to frustrate the others too. I would hate to see things go downhill for him socially, so

I wanted to touch base with you to see if we can figure something out that could help him? [It's a guiding question, based on partnership, designed to evoke change talk]

MOTHER: What kinds of things does he do?

TEACHER: Sometimes it's little things, like talking during work time or jumping out of line. And while sometimes he responds to me when I redirect him, other times he has more trouble following direction. [Notice the difference between "he has more trouble following direction" and "he doesn't listen to me."] Also, there are times when he'll get in disagreements with kids, like he might take their book or pen, he may even get physical with them in line. Nothing drastic, just some pushing and shoving. [Information provided in a fairly objective way]

MOTHER: And what about the other kids? I bet Jimmy's not the only one doing stuff. [She becomes naturally defensive]

TEACHER: Certainly, he's by no means the only student I need to talk with or redirect at times. I felt it was important though to reach out to you because I feel like the remainder of his year could potentially go really well if we can help him with his behavior. [Maintaining focus on partnership]

MOTHER: Of course I want him to improve. [Change talk] What do you need from me?

TEACHER: I would be interested in hearing what sorts of things tend to work for you at home with managing his behavior. And if you'd like, I could also share some things that have been effective in the classroom. [Eliciting mother's ideas on what works at home]

MOTHER: Well, I try not to let Jimmy get away with much. He really likes movies so we have a routine where if we don't have any problems and he does his homework and chores, then we usually watch something together at night. When he's out of hand I will try time-outs and sending him to his room. That works sometimes but other times it can take a while for him to settle down.

TEACHER: So in general he responds well to clear limits and likes having some quality time with you watching a movie. And time-out works occasionally although sometimes he takes a while to get himself together. [Reflection]

MOTHER: It does sound similar.

Commentary

The conversation proceeds from there where the teacher and mother exchange ideas on what might work. In the language of MI, they evoke change talk together. A number of classroom strategies could work at this juncture, and what specific behavior management strategies they agree to implement might be fairly easy to agree on. The aim here is to illustrate rapid engagement and evoking the mother's openness to change. Of course, some parents might push back much harder than this mother did, and this would be a call to work more on engagement as an investment in hopefully more constructive conversations in the future.

> *In the language of MI, the teacher and the mother evoke change talk together.*

Across Ages

The MI spirit concept of *partnership* is particularly relevant when working with parents of children of any age. Although all students benefit from those who support their natural tendencies toward growth, older students have more direct control over their choices and performance. During collaborative conversations with parents of older students, teachers can be curious about both the parent's and the student's roles at home in creating an environment conducive for healthy development and learning.

Scenario 12.2. Report Card: Unhappy Student, Frustrated Parent

Scenario

A teacher wants to make the most of the few minutes he has with a frustrated and cross parent and his 10-year-old daughter, in a discussion of a report card. It could be tricky. Rachel is falling behind and her classroom behavior is not ideal. The father looks furious.

What the Scenario Illustrates

Using MI skills to find agreement about the way ahead: The core skills can help the conversation go in the right direction, hopefully with a payoff in the classroom in the following days. The goal of these short conversations is to strengthen the motivation of students to improve; it might also help prevent a power struggle and discord between the child and the parent.

Setting Your Sights

The teacher has been concerned about a notable drop in this student's performance. He has some ideas, and is hoping that her father will be supportive. Aware that this might turn out less than constructive, he sets his sights on engagement and decides to make sure that he elicits the student's ideas about what happened with her grades and what she plans to do going forward. In a nutshell, that's what MI is designed to achieve—change plans that are owned by the student.

Traps to Avoid

Losing the child's voice: Conversations involving parents and children can be challenging, particularly when there is "bad news" to deliver. The student can easily view this as a coordinated effort to control her behavior at home and at school, and fade into the background, passively listening (or not!). The parent often wants to generate some motivation and specific strategies for change. The adults could easily take over here, delivering one take-home point after another; or the teacher might get caught in a family conflict. The task is to deliver feedback supportively, based on engagement, and then evoke the student's own ideas on where to go from here.

In Practice

The teacher greets Rachel and her father as they enter the classroom.

> TEACHER: Hello, Rachel. And nice to see you again, sir. Here's the report card. I'll give you a moment to look it over. I would like to talk about it after if that's OK. [Rachel and her father look over the report card and exchange a few muttered comments with each other.]
>
> FATHER: Not looking so good last term, huh?
>
> TEACHER: There was a change from the previous two terms, which concerns you. [Reflection]
>
> FATHER: Absolutely. This kind of performance is unacceptable. She's just not applying herself like she should.
>
> STUDENT: (*Rolls her eyes, looks down at the floor*)
>
> TEACHER: So Dad is clearly concerned about you, and you don't look too pleased either Rachel. Having gotten to know you

this year I suspect you're not too happy about the report card. [Reflection of nonverbal behavior]

STUDENT: No, not really.

TEACHER: School is important to you. [Reflection]

STUDENT: Usually it is.

FATHER: Then what happened? It's like all of a sudden you stopped caring.

STUDENT: I told you, Dad, I just got behind and couldn't catch up.

FATHER: Couldn't catch up or didn't want to?

TEACHER: There are several ideas about what went wrong. Some of it might have been at our end. I've also been wondering if there was a class or two that got more difficult for you Rachel? [Teacher, noting tension between Rachel and her father, gently reflects their having "several ideas" and transitions to open question for Rachel about where she had trouble]

STUDENT: Math did. I didn't get it at all.

FATHER: Then why didn't you get help? You didn't say anything until it was too late.

STUDENT: I don't know Dad, OK? You keep asking me the same question. I just didn't.

TEACHER: You are both frustrated with it. Rachel, I was hoping we could talk a bit about what you think can be different this term. We could talk for a few minutes now or if you'd prefer to talk tomorrow we could meet then. [Reflection about both of their frustration; supporting Rachel's autonomy]

STUDENT: Now is fine.

TEACHER: So you are not pleased with how you did this term. Doing well in school is important to you and you seem to be frustrated with all of the attention paid to the grades you got. How do you see yourself turning things around? [Reflection; Affirmation; Open question to elicit change talk]

STUDENT: I guess I need to make sure I don't fall behind in math. [Change talk]

TEACHER: You've mentioned that a few times. It's important for you. [Reflection]

STUDENT: I guess I could try and stay after school once or twice. [Change talk]

FATHER: I'm not sure if once or twice will cut it. The way these grades were you may need a lot more help than that.

TEACHER: So how much help you'll need is a question. Could I share an idea about that? [Asking permission] (*Both Rachel and her father nod their heads.*) I'm pretty sure your math teacher will be happy to meet with you a couple of times next week to review the unit that gave you trouble. Maybe after those two sessions you'll have a better idea if you need more help than that or not. What do you think about that option? [Providing information with the request to hear their reaction]

Commentary

Conversations with students and parents are challenging when there is tension in the air. In a short period of time the teacher in this dialogue reflected the concerns of both father and daughter, and framed the discussion around Rachel's motivation to do well in school. He did not take the tempting route of providing her with a bunch of solutions. He elicited her ideas, and kept her actively engaged.

Across Ages

Occasionally well-meaning parents of younger students can come down hard on them or take on responsibility for their children's' work. It can help to evoke how parents handle this balance while giving feedback, with permission, about developmentally appropriate expectations. Parents of older students may feel they are more in the dark as to the progress or expectations of their sons or daughters. Applying an elicit–provide–elicit strategy can help maintain a collaborative relationship with parents.

Scenario 12.3. Angry Parent:
"I'm Very Upset with This Situation"

Scenario

A parent comes into the administrator's office, very angry. The child could be of any age. The conversation can lurch downward off the back of an ill-timed or poorly worded response, or improve and turn toward resolution. What not to say can be just as important as what the administrator does say.

What the Scenario Illustrates

Using the core skill of reflection to deescalate tension: Reflection can even turn the conversation purposefully in another direction. Reflections make it clear that being upset is a legitimate response and that feeling heard is critical.

Setting Your Sights

Administrators know that when a parent is upset it means he or she cares about wanting the situation to work for his or her child, and that is something to affirm. Being open to change is a two-way street and hearing what upsets parents can be valuable for an educational institution. Transforming strong emotion into productive actions is quite a challenge.

> *When a parent is upset it means he or she cares, and that is something to affirm.*

Traps to Avoid

Reinforcing discord: Avoid the trap of escalating the parent's emotional reaction by arguing or trying to justify what caused the reaction in the first place. This will only create further discord and diminish the possibility of changing the parent's reaction and coming to a reasonable understanding. Definitely avoid giving the parent a lecture about his or her parenting. You will be looking for trouble!

In Practice: Thumbs Up or Thumbs Down?

Below is a statement by Parent A and a set of four possible administrator or teacher responses. Which responses are consistent with MI (thumbs up)? Which are not (thumbs down)? Consider how they all take the conversation in different directions. The parent will often respond to the very last few words you use. Make your selections and then compare them with our explanations in the answer key at the end of the chapter. Statements by Parents B and C follow, each with a set of possible responses to select from.

Parent A

"I can't afford to take off from work to come to deal with the fact that kids pick on Kyle. So he gets in fights."

Responses

1. "This situation is upsetting, particularly because you have to take time off work, which creates a real hardship."
2. "It's particularly frustrating for you to have to come and meet because Kyle is being picked on."
3. "Ultimately, as the parent, you are responsible for Kyle and I'm sure that you understand, as much of an inconvenience as it is to come, fighting is a serious infraction regardless of the cause."
4. "You wish you didn't have to deal with this whole inconvenience and wish situations like this would get resolved before they turn into fights."

Parent B

"It is upsetting to come home and find my child distraught because this school allows kids to post slanderous things about other children. It has got to stop!"

Responses

1. "I hear you, but unfortunately we have no control over what kids do, we can't monitor them all the time, how could we?"
2. "It's disturbing to see your child so upset because of the action of other students. Figuring out how to deal with students who post cruel things about others is really important."
3. "You've come down here determined to do something about this, and bring it to our attention."
4. "If parents would only come to the PTA meetings we could resolve this, it usually involves back-and-forth postings by the students, and blaming is not helpful."

Parent C

"The gym teacher hates my daughter; I can't believe she's getting an F because she refuses to wear gym clothes. Other kids do the same and pass."

Responses

1. "It seems unfair that your daughter would get an F when you feel that there are others who do the same and are passing."
2. "Some students are embarrassed about their bodies and do not

like wearing gym clothes, so that is probably why your daughter does that, yet it is required for all students. Have you talked to her about that so she can pass?"
3. "You care that your daughter does well in school, and it's frustrating that she is getting an F in gym. We can try to find out regarding grading consistency in gym; in addition, is there anything that would make it easier for your daughter to meet the requirements?"
4. "I understand why she could be self-conscious wearing gym clothes, that's because she's probably a bit overweight. If that is the case, there is a program that meets after school for students to help them go on a diet and eat right and that would surely help."

We are not suggesting that there is always a correct MI-consistent response to every tricky situation. However, the progress of conversations about change can hang on a small moment in which you make things better or worse. Reflection is a very safe way to progress in a conversation. In MI reflection serves two purposes: to help the other feel understood, and to point the conversation in a positive direction.

Answer Key

Responses to Parent A

1. Thumbs up: Reflection. The parent will feel acknowledged, and probably talk about the strain of leaving work.
2. Thumbs up: Reflection. The parent will feel acknowledged, and probably talk about Kyle being picked on.
3. Thumbs down: It may be true, but the parent will not feel heard, discord will increase, and you are likely to hear something like "Yes, but . . . ," followed by a counterargument.
4. Thumbs up: Reflection. The parent will feel acknowledged, and probably talk about preventing fights.

Responses to Parent B

1. Thumbs down: An initial attempt to understand the parent's perspective is followed by an MI-inconsistent counterargument, likely to leave the parent feeling frustrated.
2. Thumbs up: Reflection. The parent will feel heard and probably appreciate the rapid and efficient focus on what to do about the problem.

3. Thumbs up: Reflection and an affirmation. The parent will feel understood.
4. Thumbs down: A counterargument, which includes an implied criticism of the parent. Likely to elicit further argument.

Responses to Parent C

1. Thumbs up: Reflection. It captures what the parent has said and is likely to evoke a reply like, "Yes, exactly."
2. Thumbs down: Trying to explain the cause by providing information without permission, followed by a closed question that is confrontational.
3. Thumbs up: An affirmation, followed by an MI-adherent statement concerning the allegation and an open question to elicit possible solutions.
4. Thumbs down: Judgmental and presumptuous about student's weight being a concern; bypasses parent's concern; inappropriate and premature talk about remedial action.

FOCUSED APPLICATIONS

In Part III we take a closer look at the application of MI to four aspects of the student experience that are important and challenging for students and educators alike: bullying, working with at-risk students, dropout prevention, and postsecondary transitions. Other topics, like the use of MI for students struggling with mental health problems, likely will emerge as targets for the use of MI, because of the benefits of harnessing student strengths and wisdom to find solutions that make sense to them. Research and program development is underway with some promising results so far (Naar-King & Suarez, 2011).

We shall devote a chapter to each of the above four topics. We provide an overview of the challenge; then we present our views on how MI can be helpful to support students involved with bullying, those who face multiple difficulties with their personal development, those who may be considering dropping out, and students who are successfully completing school yet may be unsure what to do next.

A temptation with each of the four chapters to follow is to view the topic as a problem in students. In truth, these difficulties manifest in a broader context of relationship building within a school. The more effort put into this on a daily basis, the less likely it will be that a problem like bullying will raise its head.

Bullying

My pain may be the reason for somebody's laugh. But my laugh must never be the reason for somebody's pain.
—*Charlie Chaplin*

Hurtful words and actions, unfortunately, are quite common in schools. Bullying has often been considered a natural part of growing up or something that builds character. However, most educators agree that bullying has the potential for serious long-term negative consequences. The stakes are high.

While most schools likely have policies in place designed to curtail bullying, effective response remains a challenge. Frequently, schools enact a range of responses, from formal schoolwide programs to informal suggestions of how teachers and administrators should manage incidents that occur. As with any response to student behavior, it is important to consider how educators can engage in helpful conversations with their students about bullying.

One of the many challenges when responding to bullying is the involvement of multiple students, whose needs may vary considerably. On the surface the solutions might seem straightforward: for the bully, "Cut it out!"; for the victim, "Tell a grownup" or "Just ignore it." But these are more examples of the well-intentioned righting reflex in action. As any educator can likely attest, the situations are often too complex for such responses to be effective.

Bullying is not simply a problem of behavior, with a perpetrator(s) and his or her victim. It is often a reflection of how people treat each other throughout a school. Not simply student-to-student, but adult-to-student and adult-to-adult, parents included. We are not suggesting anyone is to blame; rather, educators should look beyond student interactions when seeking solutions to bullying. It's paramount to foster a culture of respect for all members of the school community, in which building good relationships all around will prevent episodes from arising in the first place.

Bullying is not simply a problem of a perpetrator and victim.

In this chapter we briefly discuss the challenge of bullying and how MI might help bolster the ways school personnel respond.

The Challenge

While there are many definitions of bullying (Olweus, 1993; Rigby, 2013), several commonalities to these definitions exist, including:

- Bullying involves physical (e.g., hitting, kicking), verbal (e.g., teasing), and/or social acts (e.g., purposeful exclusion, spreading rumors) that are intentionally hurtful. These acts can occur face-to-face, in written form, and electronically. The latter is commonly referred to as "cyberbullying."
- The acts are repetitive rather than isolated incidents.
- A power imbalance exists between a bully and his or her victim, in that it is difficult for the victim to defend him- or herself because of physical limitations or differences in social status.
- Often the perpetrator(s) enjoys the experience and the victim feels oppressed.

The prevalence of bullying has also received much attention from researchers. While there are many challenges in determining precisely how big a problem bullying is (see Cornell & Bandyopadhyay, 2010, for a discussion of bullying assessment), we present estimates from a meta-analysis conducted by Cook, Williams, Guerra, and Kim (2010). The following rates are from a compilation of school-based studies on bullying presented across ages and gender for select countries (see Cook et al., 2010, for a more detailed review):

- United States: 17.9% bullies; 21.5% victims; and 7.7% bully-victims
- England: 15.0% bullies; 23.9% victims; and 7.9% bully-victims
- Norway: 6.0% bullies; 11.3% victims; and 7.2% bully-victims
- Australia: 15.8% bullies; 32.5% victims; and 9.0% bully-victims
- South Korea: 11.3% bullies; 7.9% victims; and 7.2% bully-victims
- South Africa: 22.0% bullies; 22.9% victims; data unavailable for bully-victims

As you can see, these estimates vary widely. However, based on this research, it is quite clear that bullying is a phenomenon that cuts across geographical regions and cultures. Educators worldwide are responding to the challenge bullying presents.

What happens to children that experience bullying? Not just the victims, but what of those who perpetrate bullying on others? Or those children that experience both sides; as bully and victim? Much has been written and studied about the outcomes of bullying, and our purpose here is not to review this extensive literature. However, we present the following simply to highlight why bullying prevention and intervention are so important:

- Children ages 4–10 involved in any form of bullying (particularly chronic victims and those both bullies and victims) were at significantly greater risk of developing suicidal ideation and suicidal/self-injurious behavior, *by age 11* (Winsper, Lereya, Zanarini, & Wolke, 2012).
- Children ages 9–11 who experienced an episode of bullying victimization at the beginning of the school year were at significantly greater risk later in the year for developing depression, anxiety, abdominal pain, bedwetting, or "feeling tense" than children who did not (Fekkes, Pijpers, Fredriks, Vogels, & Verloove-Vanhorick, 2006).
- Children in grades 6–10 (United States; approximately ages 10–15) classified as having bullied others or as being both a bully/victim were associated with significantly poorer academic achievement (Nansel et al., 2001).
- Children ages 9–16 classified as a victim or both bully and victim were at significantly greater risk of developing depression

and anxiety disorders in young adulthood than children that did not meet victim or bully-victim classification (Copeland, Wolke, Angold, & Costello, 2013).

These are just a small handful of studies that demonstrate the immediate and long-term negative outcomes that students exposed to bullying are more likely to endure. In response to these sobering facts, schools across the globe are responding with programs designed to prevent bullying from festering within their classrooms and corridors. What are some of these programs and how can MI help?

Common Responses to Bullying

School professionals often respond to bullying in two ways (Rigby & Bauman, 2010): (1) schoolwide bullying prevention efforts, often with an additional overall goal of improving school climate; and (2) focused interventions that respond to incidents of bullying between specific students. Schoolwide efforts that are thoroughly implemented can reduce bullying by roughly 20% (Ttofi & Farrington, 2011). Examples of schoolwide programs include the Olweus Bullying Prevention Program (OBPP; Olweus, 1993), Bully Proofing Your School (BPYS; Garrity, Jens, Porter, Sager, & Short-Camilli, 1994), and Creating a Peaceful School Learning Environment (CAPSLE; Twemlow et al., 2001). (See Jimerson, Swearer, & Espelage, 2010, for more discussion on these and other programs.) While common goals exist for reducing bullying in school, such programs have some fairly distinct areas of emphasis where MI could fit quite nicely.

For instance, OBPP has a specific focus on training teachers to conduct classroomwide and individual conversations with students and parents (Olweus & Limber, 2010). The classroomwide discussions are prevention efforts that highlight the rules against bullying, as well as conducting problem-solving exercises, among other topics. The individual conversations involve "serious talks" (Olweus & Limber, 2010, p. 382) between teachers, students, and parents about specific bullying situations that occur throughout the year. Aspects of the BPYS program emphasize creating a "caring community" (Porter, Plog, Jens, Garrity, & Sager, 2010, p. 432) of adults and students when responding to the bully, as well as deemphasizing punishment in favor of prosocial education.

The second approach, responding to actual incidents of bullying, most commonly revolves around punishment (Rigby, 2013), ranging from stern conversation, to an afterschool detention, or an in-school or out-of-school suspension. Rigby (2013) lists several nonpunitive approaches, both for one-on-one bullying situations, such as mediation and restorative programs, as well as an intervention to address a group of students bullying another student, known as the method of shared concern. These nonpunitive approaches tend to involve conversations aimed toward understanding the situation from all points of view, resolving long-standing conflicts, or eliciting empathy from the perpetrator(s) toward the victim. (For a discussion of MI and nonpunitive interventions, see Chapter 14, "At-Risk Students.")

> *The most common response to bullying is punishment.*

How MI Can Help

All of these responses involve conversations at some level. While many of you will recognize some natural contradictions between relying on punitive methods and employing MI, we would argue that there can be MI-consistent ways of having a conversation with a student found to be bullying while maintaining a strengths-based, collaborative position. However, the nonpunitive methods are more natural fits with MI, as they explicitly use engagement and evocative efforts with the involved student(s).

How would MI look in practice? Consider the following situation:

A teacher meets with 14-year-old Johnny after class about an exchange the teacher observed between Johnny and a classmate, Tim. The teacher saw Johnny making fun of Tim's hair, with other peers laughing at Tim as well. As Tim appeared to get angry, the teacher walked over and asked everyone to get back to work.

As we've suggested throughout this book, a helpful way to approach the conversation with Johnny would be to start from his perspective, with engaging. What does he think is going on? Does he think this is friendly banter? Maybe he believes Tim is just "playing along." Educators are often well attuned to the social nuances that exist in their schools and have their own answers to these sorts of questions. Yet coming into the conversation with curiosity about Johnny's perspective can secure a solid relational footing for subsequent discussions about change.

It would be understandable to want to approach Johnny ready to teach him a lesson. The righting reflex could lead in any number of directions, such as a recitation of school policy, threats about detention or suspension, or even a plea to "be nice" or "make friends." These can be important points in some situations, yet the risk of creating discord and eliminating the opportunity to engage with Jonny is strong. Let's see how MI might fit:

TEACHER: Johnny, can I talk with you about something?

STUDENT: (*Leaves group of friends and walks over slightly annoyed.*) Yeah?

TEACHER: I'd like to talk with you about what happened a few minutes ago when I had to ask everyone to get back to work. Seems like you and Tim haven't been getting along lately.

STUDENT: (*Shrugs shoulders.*) I guess not.

TEACHER: What's that about I wonder? [Open question]

STUDENT: I don't know. We just don't like each other I guess.

TEACHER: You're not sure what it's about. [Reflection]

STUDENT: Not really.

TEACHER: Kind of hard for everyone to get along with each other all the time. [Reflection]

STUDENT: (*Nods head*)

TEACHER: It does seem as if you get along well with most everyone else in class. Almost like you're a bit of a leader. [Affirmation, despite Johnny's role as the "bully"]

STUDENT: I don't know about that, I just have lots of friends I guess.

TEACHER: It sure seems that way. There is one specific part of what happened today that I would like to hear your thoughts about. I noticed that you were making fun of Tim's hair, which seemed to get some of the others laughing too. Tell me more about that part.

STUDENT: It wasn't a big deal or anything. We were just having some fun.

TEACHER: OK, sure. I've seen you guys have fun quite a bit together. I wonder if Tim felt the same way?

STUDENT: Maybe. He's laughed about those things before.

TEACHER: It's hard to tell sometimes. [Reflection]

STUDENT: Maybe he was in a bad mood or something.

TEACHER: Maybe so. I do want to share a concern I had about what I saw and hear what you think about it. It looked like you guys were teasing Tim and he was upset about it. Like you were bullying him. [Said in a neutral tone]

STUDENT: But it wasn't that big a deal. He takes things so seriously sometimes.

TEACHER: It's not always easy to tell when someone is ready to joke around. [Reflection] What do you think you might do different next time so that he doesn't get his feelings hurt and you don't risk getting in trouble for something? [Evoking change talk]

STUDENT: I guess I can just leave him alone. [Change talk]

TEACHER: So you might try keeping your attention on your friends or your classwork. Sounds like you have a plan. Can I ask you, what do you know about rules against bullying in our school?

STUDENT: Don't you get a detention or something?

TEACHER: Yes, that would likely happen if it continued. [Presented *without* a threatening tone]

The MI-consistent conversation continues a little longer, providing Johnny an opportunity to reflect on his behavior, with clarity about consequences yet without excessive threats of punishment or negative judgment of Johnny's character. By initiating a process of Johnny embracing the importance of not making fun of others, the teasing is less likely to continue.

And of course there is Tim, the victim, who could benefit from an opportunity to talk with his teacher about the incident. Such a conversation would involve engaging with Tim by acknowledging his feelings and affirming his strengths, with statements such as: "You know what it feels like to be laughed at and you're careful not to do that to others" or "It's hard to know what to say to a group of kids calling you names."

The righting reflex could be just as strong with Tim, as most teachers' want to be helpful and likely have plenty of ideas of what Tim might do to change his circumstance with respect to the bullying. However, when using MI, we would encourage the use of evocative questions and reflections exploring what Tim has already tried and what he thinks might work now before providing "solutions." The teacher can certainly share ideas and give feedback, just with permission and with a keen eye to how Tim receives the input. What does Tim imagine would happen if he tries one strategy versus another? Is he confident he'll succeed, or maybe he's worried about reprisals? These are all important points to wonder about that may not be apparent if trying to provide solutions without appreciating their impact.

In responding to bullying, use evocative questions and reflections.

Such MI-consistent conversations may be enough if bullying incidents were isolated events. However, bullying can create a peer culture of putdowns, therefore making opportunities for broader learning through classwide discussions or restorative justice circles. Allowing bullying to fester can contribute to toxic stress, which can undermine learning and other school outcomes.

Conclusion

Bullying is a serious matter that often impacts students' health and academic performance, and in rare yet tragic cases leads to suicide or revenge violence. Bullying may also be an indicator of a school climate that devalues certain members of its community. Using MI as a way to address bullying incidents, with individuals, pairs, or groups of students, may be a valuable way for teachers, administrators, or other adults to intervene quickly, and as part of a broader effort to integrate MI with other approaches. MI-based intervention efforts can help the student who is a bully, a victim, or both by recruiting the inner resources of students to act from and build more positive strengths, with bullies potentially gaining valuable empathy skills and victims learning how to respond more effectively.

At-Risk Students

MI Integrated with Other Approaches

Beware how you take away hope from any
human being.

—*Oliver Wendell Holmes*

Any method for turning around the lives of at-risk students carries a warning: If it's not a holistic effort, with hope for a better life at its core, then disappointment could follow. There are multiple factors that place a student at risk or position them for success. Hence the focus of this chapter: MI *integrated* with other approaches to better the lives of vulnerable young people.

Students can fail to get the most out of school, lose hope, even give up, often at a crucial time in their development. What we do in school can contribute to either failure or success. Front-line teachers are critically important in the way they develop relationships, spot problems early, and encourage students to make the best of what they can be. So are professionals with more specialist roles in helping students with change, such as behavioral consultants, social workers, or nurses. Strong relationships and constructive conversations informed by MI can help students to flourish.

> *If it's not a holistic effort disappointment could follow.*

The Challenge

Working effectively with students considered "at risk" is one of the biggest challenges faced by educators. It absorbs countless hours of effort, and outcomes are often disappointing. The most deprived communities often bear the brunt. Students who are victims of racism, poverty, and social exclusion, who lack adequate social–emotional support, or who have disabilities are particularly vulnerable. Students with special needs are often the ones most at risk, with over a quarter of them apparently giving up on high school (Test et al., 2009).

Structures and controls are needed to create a safe learning environment, yet a reliance on punishment can increase negative outcomes (Lee, Cornell, Gregory, & Fan, 2011). The "school-to-prison pipeline" is an unfortunate reality; vulnerable circumstances plus outright discrimination in some instances put certain students at extremely high risk. For instance, studies in the United States show that children of color are more than twice as likely as their white peers to be suspended, expelled, or arrested for the same misconduct at school (Losen, 2011). Those eligible for special education make up only 9% of public school students yet are roughly 33% of youth in correction facilities (Kim, Losen, & Hewitt, 2010).

It is usually easy to spot the markers of students who are at risk: lower than expected academic grades, failures, poor social skills, aggression, truancy, social isolation, learning problems, health or mental health matters. What to do about these students is the challenge.

Principles of Good Practice

One starting point is to consider the effect of the label "at risk." It might seem innocuous enough when viewed as an isolated description, but the label often creates a vicious circle: the more students are viewed and spoken to as a "problem," the more they internalize this view of themselves, and act accordingly. This self-fulfilling prophecy has been studied from various angles.

The label "at risk" is often self-fulfilling.

In the classic Pygmalion studies, students completed a fake test to determine who would excel in future years. Teachers received the names of 20% of students randomly selected as the "bloomers." After 8 months those so-called bloomers showed higher gains, and teachers rated them as more curious, better adjusted, happier, and less needy than the control group (Rosenthal & Jacobson, 1968; Baker & Crist, 1971). Labels can be counterproductive when they influence adult expectations of students, which are then easily internalized by students, particularly the case in less autonomous classrooms (Conzolino, 2013). Students interpret the diverse range of adult signals that include body language, attitude, and actions like blaming, punishing, or ignoring. And although alternative terms such as "vulnerable," "marginalized," or "opportunity youth" might help, a key variable regardless of label is the care adults give to their interactions with students.

What, then, are some principles of good practice? Running through a wide range of programs are some common threads that could be well suited to integration with MI, and thus potentially improve outcomes for these students. Here is a list of some of the most salient:

- *Early intervention.* It's obvious yet critical to catch problems early before they become harder to remediate, monitoring continuously from the early years through high school with necessary supports made available. This highlights the valuable role of the front-line teacher.
- *Autonomy support.* Students need structure, but shaming, issuing fines, inducing boredom, or mandating actions without inherent value can unwittingly demotivate students and lead to their further alienation and poor outcomes (DeCharmes et al., 1976; Reeve, 1996; Vansteenkiste, Mouratidis, & Lens, 2005). Engagement is unlikely if they feel manipulated, sense they are powerless, or fail to internalize the broader lessons offered to them. Put simply, students need to own their decisions about their attitudes, reactions, and behavior change.
- *Social–emotional skill development.* This means many things, including but not limited to helping students to express their thoughts and feelings, as well as improving their executive functioning skills, such as planning ahead and regulating emotions.
- *Behavior support.* Similar to social–emotional development, the focus here is to support the learning of self-regulation skills, which can often lead to more positive attitudes. Research findings show that differences in school performance between demographic groups can fade by focusing on students' attitudes and behaviors (Farrington et al., 2012).
- *Strengths-based approach.* Emphasis on strengths sits beneath many effective programs, increasing hope and self-efficacy.

Expressing empathy is particularly valuable with students with many interrelated problems.

• *Fostering healthy relationships.* Teachers are challenged with limited time to interact with students. Yet research suggests the importance of adult–student relationships in ameliorating risk factors for students with special needs as they transition into and navigate through school (Sinclair, Christensen, & Thurlow, 2005; Dunn, Chambers, & Rabren, 2004; Kortering, Braziel, & Tompkins, 2002). Students need to feel that there is a helpful adult they can count on in the school who cares about them and their academic performance.

How to weave these threads of good practice into conversations that make a difference is where MI might help.

How MI Can Help

MI can be used as a form of individual counseling or in groups (Wagner & Ingersoll, 2012), and by a wide range of professionals like administrators, security officers, mentors, or coaches. Given the flexibility of MI, a broader goal exists: to improve the quality of conversations about change throughout a school. MI is strengths-based, a way of talking about change that fosters a healthy relationship, generates clarity, and fosters hope as students say what they feel, think, and focus on change. The use of MI to evoke students' thoughts and feelings in favor of behavior change is its defining characteristic. It is based on harnessing the power of positive attitudes within students themselves and focusing on those behaviors that schools have the biggest challenge knowing how to approach.

> *MI helps us evoke students' thoughts and feelings in favor of behavior change.*

"Change talk" can be about making amends for misdeeds, becoming more mindful of emotional reactions, or making decisions to improve the self. It can be about participating in activities like tutoring, mentoring, counseling, sports, clubs, joining a leadership program, or even the more subtle yet transformative decision to view the self differently. All these decisions can have the potential of reducing risk for students, and they take place every day. How might MI fit with everyday programs and practice in school? That's what the remainder of this chapter will turn to.

Nonpunitive Approaches

As strengths-based, restorative, and nonpunitive approaches gain ground in many schools, MI can be a component that enhances the overall effort. Restorative justice is one such method that attempts to resolve peer conflicts between students that have been victimized by other students, without focusing solely on punishing the perpetrator(s). A central aspect of this approach is the restorative justice talking circle, a conversation between victim and perpetrator, guided by an adult facilitator. MI can be used as an effective communication style both before the talking circle as a way to increase students' engagement with the restorative process, and during the talking circle where skillful guidance can maximize the impact of this approach to conflict resolution.

There are other nonpunitive approaches that may find blending with MI useful, including peer mediation or peer juries. These require conversations drawing on empathic, reflective listening skills. Anyone working with at-risk students will likely find they respond well to MI. It is a welcome contrast to punishment, and will likely conclude with a more permanent and positive outcome. By using MI's nonjudgmental conversational approach, students have a chance to think clearly without feeling compelled to defend their behavior. Rather than creating discord with punishment and feelings of resentment, students can feel heard. Thus they are more likely to own their behavior leading to a commitment to change.

> *In an MI conversation, students have a chance to think clearly.*

Experiential Learning

The use of experiential education, which uses games and initiatives to nurture trust and respect while helping students develop their social emotional skills (Frank, 2013), can be an important component to blend with MI. It is suggested that the rise of anxiety and depression in children is linked to a decline in personal control, suggesting that play can be a useful remedy (Gray, 2011; Robinson, 2014). Blending playfulness with MI has been a model used by one of the authors for nearly a decade in working with at risk students (see Box 14.1).

Cognitive–Behavioral Approaches

Some programs that use cognitive-behavioral interventions in schools may find that MI can help students increase their willingness to develop

BOX 14.1. Blending MI with Experiential Education

In a university–school partnership in Chicago, a colleague and I (R. R.) brought graduate students, trained in blending MI and experiential learning, to a high school to work with "at-risk" youth who were on the "hot list" (i.e., the most vulnerable young people). On three Fridays during regular class time these students were encouraged to spend the first hour in playful experiential activities building cooperation, safety, trust, and a sense of community. Trust-building activities were difficult for students as the street violence they experienced had left traumatic scars. This was followed by one-on-one MI sessions. Meeting success, this effort has continued for 4 years. The social worker in charge of referring students was so impressed with the results of these sessions that she decided to attend training sessions in MI and during the session mentioned that of the many programs at the school, this one was the one that showed results. A student was overheard sharing with another student what it involved and said, "It's about games to work together, getting stuff off your chest, and focusing on your goals." Group discussions help process what was learned and integrate concepts like "name it to tame it (controlling anger)," "effort builds intelligence," and "the ripple effect of trustworthiness." The evaluation has shown increases in grade point averages, decreases in failures, better attendance, and a higher graduation rate for participating seniors.

the necessary skills to resolve conflicts or find solutions to barriers. Programs like check and connect (Sinclair, Christensen, & Thurlow, 2005), deep brain learning (Brendtro, Mitchell, & McCall, 2009), changing mind-sets (Dweck, 2006), and others designed to increase students' understanding of their brains may be enhanced if students have resolved their ambivalence and feel personally responsible for creating change through the use of MI. This blending has been useful in other fields that use cognitive-behaviorial therapy (Miller & Rollnick, 2013, p. 373).

In the Classroom

Although research finds that student-centered, autonomy-supportive classrooms are best at generating student interest, a mistaken belief exists that to do so runs counter to providing clear structure for students. The most effective classrooms are ones that provide clear structure *and* support student autonomy (Jang, Reeve, & Deci, 2010). There are various student-centered models for this population that could work well with MI, particularly since the common thread among these practices is having students take a central role in shaping their educational pathway (Toshalis & Nakkula, 2012; Hinton, Fischer, & Glennon, 2012). Practices like active learning or therapeutic arts integration that involve expressing creativity and emotions (the brain's save button) can help students learn and change (see Box 14.2).

> *The most effective classrooms provide clear structure and support student autonomy.*

Conclusion

MI can be integrated with other programs to better serve at-risk students so they will be more likely to change behavior for their immediate or long-term benefit. MI brings a practical way to help schools serve at-risk students that does not threaten their autonomy. Misbehavior can be an opportunity for growth and MI can help students gain a sense of agency as they decide to change.

MI can be embedded in school practices to counter failure and provide a way of effectively addressing all students' needs while building their inner resources. Improving the quality of interactions can enhance student confidence and commitment to change. This fuels hope into action, something that can be useful in all schools.

BOX 14.2. Blending MI with Art

In Krakow, Poland, MI is integrated with art and narrative therapy to develop social skills with high school students involved in negative behaviors including aggression, violence, scapegoating or bullying, drugs, or risky sex. Students also attend workshops using MI skills to help them with aggression or self-injury and to focus on developing empathy and controlling their emotions. MI is used to enhance abilities and internal resources. (Cezary Baranski, school social worker, Krakow, Poland, October 2013, personal communication).

15

Dropout Prevention and Reengagement

Most dropouts are students who could have,
and believe they could have, succeeded in
school.
—*John M. Bridgeland, John J. DiIulio, Jr.,
and Karen Burke Morison (2006)*

Eight-year-old Justin came home from school and complained to his mother that he hated school and didn't want to go anymore. She had never liked school herself, yet she responded, "Want to or not, you have to go." Justin could have been diagnosed with attention-deficit/hyperactivity disorder or some other psychiatric condition; however, he was never evaluated. That year Justin was held back. Achievement tests indicated he was falling further and further behind. Yet, on more creative and artistic tasks, he showed interest and excelled. It was clear from most of his grades, attitude, and the interactions between home and school that he had dropped out emotionally years before he finished eighth grade. He never showed up for high school.

Rose, on the other hand, thrived in school. Since kindergarten, teachers and peers saw her as a natural leader and connected easily with her. But when she was in seventh grade, her parents divorced and her life abruptly changed. She moved and changed schools. The trajectory of her academic experience plummeted. By high school, she was utterly disengaged. She cut classes with her friends, started failing classes, and was frequently involved in disruptive behavior, resulting in a series of detentions and suspensions. Frequent meetings with the attendance office that required her mother to take time off work became commonplace that year. At the age of 16 she and some of her friends quit going to school altogether; as her mother says, Rose "chose to hang out with friends who were a bad influence."

The reasons for truancy or dropping out are unique to each student. Undoubtedly the way they feel about school, which is due in part to the way adults treat them, plays a role. This chapter focuses on the use of MI for improving retention and reengaging dropouts, including efforts to be proactive in countering cultural differences and biases that may exist toward students.

The Challenge

In the United States, over a million students in rural, urban, and suburban schools leave classrooms every year, never to come back (Datiri, 2013). The gravity of the problem is sometimes underestimated due to inaccurate graduation figures. Although graduation data suggest that retention has increased, statisticians don't always agree on the high school dropout rate; some claim that it is as high as 30% in the United States (Center for Public Education, 2010). Even the most positive on-time graduation rates suggest that at least 20% of students drop out or take longer than 4 years to graduate (Stetser & Stillwell, 2014). In European countries the percentage of dropouts varies considerably from as low as 4% in Norway and as high as 36% in Italy (Lamb, Markussen, Teese, Sandberg, & Polesel, 2010). Low-income students are at particularly high risk for dropout worldwide, with rates as high as 75% in parts of Latin America (Herrán & Van Uythem, 2001).

Society relies on schools to prepare students for the job market, with the skills needed to respond effectively to challenges. Dropouts cost society in multiple ways: increased involvement with the corrections system (police, courts, and prisons), increased likeliness of unemployment or safety-net support, higher incidences of health- and mental health-related costs, and the resulting low contribution of taxes during their lives (Alliance for Excellence in Education, 2011). Demographic researchers warn of the profound economic costs incurred by society due to dropouts if they are not reengaged back into school (Levin, 1986; Rouse, 2005; Sum, Khatiwada, & McLaughlin, 2009).

Publically funded schools are dependent on maintaining enrollment for funding allocation, as well as a measure of effectiveness. When enrollment declines due to dropout, the pressure to retain students amplifies, both to maintain budget stability and to avoid labels such as "dropout mill." Threats and mandates, while common as the pressure builds, can create less-than-optimal learning environments by undermining teacher commitment and student engagement.

The biggest hardships from dropping out are often experienced by the individual students and their families, leading to lost opportunities and unfulfilled lives. Efforts to learn from mistakes opens the possibility to help prevent students from dropping out. What follows is some compelling research on factors that contribute to the problem and suggested solutions.

Messages from Research

Contributing Factors

How students feel about school often shows up as a factor that contributes to dropping out. When students feel alienated from school, linked in part to how school personnel relate to them, dropping out is more likely (Wehlage, 1983). A survey in urban schools found a discrepancy of perception between teachers and students regarding their ability to approach a teacher about a problem. Eighty percent of teachers reported having frequent one-on-one conversations with students, while only 27% of students said they got individual attention to address issues they were concerned about, and 25% of students said that there was not any adult in their school whom they felt they could approach with a problem (What Kids Can Do, Inc., 2004).

Research shows that students who drop out are often the same ones who struggle with absenteeism, truancy, disruptive behavior in class, and delinquency (Finn, 1989). At the same time, studies indicate a relationship between punishing students for disruptive behavior and these students ultimately dropping out (Wehlage & Rutter, 1986a), with students of color tending to receive harsher consequences (Arnez, 1978; Losen, 2011; Losen & Gillespie, 2012) and experiencing higher dropout rates (Stetser & Stillwell, 2014). The cultural divide that often exists in many schools between students and educators may be a contributing factor.

To further accentuate the *systemic problem* of school dropout, some have coined the phrase "push out" as an alternative term to "drop out," to underscore the ineffective practices occasionally used to meet the needs of at-risk students. Some have argued that students are even told to leave school and/or treated in ways that make them feel compelled to do so in some situations (Arnez, 1978; Kelly, 1993; Tuck, 2012). The behavior of adults that unwittingly strips students of autonomy can lead to the creation of intentions to drop out (Vallerand, Fortier, & Guay, 1997).

Suggested Solutions

Dropout prevention experts universally advocate for improved efforts to create community and a sense of belonging (Dynarski et al., 2008; Orfield, 2004, Wehlage & Rutter, 1986b; Newmann, 1981; Reid, 1981). Some of the specific recommendations for schools to improve retention and reduce absenteeism include:

- Cooperative relationships between students and staff (Newmann, 1981)
- Teacher interest in students (Wehlage & Rutter, 1986b)
- Efforts to help reduce feelings of alienation (Reid, 1981; Newmann, 1981)
- Building a community of support to help students face academic challenges and deal with personal issues (Wehlage, 1989)
- Helping students have clear and consistent goals (Ford & Nichols, 1987, as cited in Finn, 1989)
- Voluntary student involvement in policy and management decisions (Newmann, 1981)
- Countering the perception of being ineffective and powerless (Ford, 1987)
- Providing students with autonomy support, leading to their self-perception of competence and creating self-determined motivation to stay in school (Vallerand et al., 1997)

How students perform in their first year of high school is crucial (Allensworth & Easton, 2005). Students with no failures had an 83% graduation rate, those with one failure had a 60% rate, while those with two failures only had a 22% rate. The fact that 49% of students in this Chicago cohort had at least one failure suggested the need for improving how schools monitor and support students (Allensworth & Easton, 2005). The general consensus is that to help prevent dropouts, students need to have sustained relationships with adults throughout

To prevent drop outs, students need to have sustained relationships with adults.

their school experience who show interest, monitor and intervene rapidly with them when problems arise, and help them and their families overcome obstacles (Center for Public Education, 2010). Let's go back to Justin and Rose. What would have helped them increase their motivation to stay? There was likely plenty of time to work with Justin and Rose before they dropped out. Most likely, neither one seriously considered how dropping out would affect them in the future. They may have heard from others about the consequences of dropping out, but was that enough to internalize the message? If time for meaningful conversations with students are prioritized, would students like Justin and Rose stay in school?

How MI Can Help

As an evidence-based practice for behavior change, MI can be a tool to help meet many of the recommendations of researchers to encourage students to stay in school. It provides a means to meet students' psychological needs, by focusing on student–educator relationships, as a mechanism to help build communities of support, and creating a sense of belonging, while allowing for more student decision making and autonomy. MI can be a way to support how students feel about themselves in relation to school as well as how to structure support for students. It can provide an approach for adults (or peer mentors) to talk with students so they align their decisions with their goals in a manner that allows them to own their decisions. Research has shown that students prioritize their own reasons for attending school over external efforts to compel them to stay (DeCharmes et al., 1976; Vallerand & Bissonnette, 1992).

MI can provide a way to intervene early to deal with attendance or academic deficiencies to support getting back on track or reengaging dropouts in a way that allows them to resolve their ambivalence and own their decisions so that they keep their commitments. MI conversations can help students think clearly about their choices without pressure or judgment, providing a way to problem-solve to overcome obstacles. The link between first-semester academic failure and lower high school graduation rates 4 years

MI conversations provide a way to problem-solve to overcome obstacles.

later, as mentioned above, makes MI a potentially valuable early warning intervention.

Instead of counting on punishment, instilling fear, or attempting to convince students while taking away choice, MI provides an alternative approach, encouraging engagement (see Box 15.1). It can replace rigid structures like zero tolerance with conversations that provide a proactive way to learn from mistakes. Engaged students create a ripple effect, countering the student peer culture that undermines the value of learning.

One common reason for dropping out given by former students is that "school was boring" (Bearden, Spencer, & Moracco, 1989; Bridgeland, DiIulio, & Morison, 2006; Tidwell, 1988). What might be a useful response to these students' complaints, without showing annoyance or downplaying the legitimacy of their perception? Boredom shows a lack of intrinsic motivation and can be code for feeling controlled or socially disengaged, and having to complete academic tasks perceived as meaningless. Understanding that boredom is related to low levels of the neurotransmitter dopamine; that the adolescent brain has lower base levels; that stress can further reduce its level; and that positive social engagement can increase it (Siegal, 2013; Cozolino, 2013) would suggest that MI may help.

Another reason former students give for dropping out is some version of "I felt like a number." This, of course, is a way of saying they feel alienated, and as the studies mentioned above argue, this has

BOX 15.1. MI for College Students

Another potential goal for MI with students is to increase the study behaviors that lead to better academic performance. Like high school students, adolescents who fail courses in the first year of college are at higher risk of dropout. In an early intervention program, Mikyta Daugherty (2003) at the University of New Mexico worked with 110 students failing early exams in a freshman psychology course—a predictor of failing the course and later leaving college. These students received either three sessions of directive advice or an MI-based approach to help engage them in a study resource center. Those in the MI condition were more likely to attend all three sessions (92% vs. 47%), completed significantly more practice quizzes, scored higher on subsequent exams, and were 43% more likely to pass the course with a C– or better.

important implications for retention. MI conversations convey genuine interest and can nurture feelings of belonging.

And here is a more "logical" explanation for giving up on school: "I wasn't getting any credits, so why stay?" Admittedly, this is a realistic after-the-fact response to academic failure. Having provisions for help, like tutors or evening school courses available, does not guarantee students will utilize them. The research suggests that this failure is often directly related to factors like attitude and behavior. Learning requires the interplay between these and cognitive factors, which are developmental and embedded in "the environment and sociocultural processes" (Farrington et al., 2012, p. 2). MI conversations can enable early intervention to support the development of attitudes and mindsets that in turn facilitate learning subject matter and academic skills.

Learning to problem-solve requires sound decision making, which can be facilitated by another person guiding the thought process. Struggling students are ambivalent about what to do and need help. MI puts the autonomy of the student at the center of the process, becoming a student-centered, differentiated approach that supports improved judgment.

> *Problem solving requires sound decision making, which you can facilitate by guiding a student's thought process.*

Using MI conversations with Justin as an 8-year-old might have helped begin the process to keep him on track. Here is a short example:

TEACHER: Justin, I notice that you seem to be a little unhappy, what's happening?

STUDENT: Nothing, it's too hard. I don't like school; it makes me mad I have to come.

TEACHER: When it comes to art and drawing, they're easy for you. You put in amazing details in your pictures and they look so real. [Affirmation]

STUDENT: I like drawing, it's my favorite thing in class.

TEACHER: And you are good at it. [Affirmation] Yet with other subjects, it can be harder.

STUDENT: I can't pay attention when José makes noise.

TEACHER: You'd like to be able to focus and that's not easy with distractions. [Reflections]

STUDENT: I try to pay attention [Change talk] but it's too hard.

TEACHER: Can I ask you if there is anything that you think might help?

STUDENT: Maybe, not sure though. I don't really know.

TEACHER: Can I suggest something that might? [Asking permission]

STUDENT: What?

TEACHER: What if I moved you to the front row, would that be OK with you?

STUDENT: Everyone is going to think I got in trouble and laugh at me.

TEACHER: What if I rearranged other students also, would that help?

STUDENT: I guess. [Change talk]

This very normal-sounding conversation is highly MI-consistent. It's a start, and if the engagement with Justin is maintained in this helpful way, the chances of him feeling less alienated will likely improve.

Rose, on the other hand, got off track due to challenges going on in her home life along with the changes that come with adolescence. She probably would be a good candidate for a conversation about returning to school. It would probably include her hopes, dreams, and how she might get there.

After being out of school for a year, Rose decided to meet with a reengagement specialist trained in MI, and the following dialogue ensued:

SPECIALIST: I want to thank you for making this appointment. I'd enjoy finding out about your life these days and what you may be thinking as you move ahead.

STUDENT: I'm not here because I want to be, I'm just tired of hearing my Mom harp at me about going to school. I'm not going back to my old school.

SPECIALIST: Going back to your school is not something you're considering, even if your Mom wants you to. [Reflection]

STUDENT: I'm so far behind, I'd be laughed at by my old classmates and I'm not about to go through that.

SPECIALIST: You wish that you could catch up on credits yet you'd feel uncomfortable there. [Reflection]

STUDENT: I don't want to be in class with new students and back in the same boring classes either.

SPECIALIST: What do you think would work for you? [Open question]

STUDENT: I'm not sure, maybe another school with students who are a bit older. [Change talk]

SPECIALIST: You're not giving up on your education. [Reflection] Tell me more.

STUDENT: Like maybe night school if I can get a job or maybe a smaller school with students more like me. [More change talk]

SPECIALIST: You're considering night school or possibly going to a second-chance school if you can. You'd like to find out about your options. [Reflections]

STUDENT: I don't know much about them. I just want to make sure I could hack it. I mean, I've been out of school for a while. I'm not sure.

SPECIALIST: You don't want to jump into it and fail. As you think ahead about dreams for yourself, where does finishing high school fit? [Open question]

STUDENT: I need to finish. I want to own my own business, not sure what yet, but I know I will probably need to go on to college. [Change talk]

SPECIALIST: You are determined to make something of yourself. It's really up to you what you think would suit you best. I'd be glad to explain more about the process for getting you enrolled if you want. [The conversation continues to increase commitment language.]

Here you can see that Rose moved quickly from not wanting to go back to her old school to being willing to consider options. That may seem unrealistic, yet since the specialist refrained from pushing her, it made it possible for her to own her own decision and move in the direction of returning to a new school.

MI to Support Culturally Diverse Students

There is a correlation between dropping out and the cultural, ethnic, and racial background of students. Although the percentages reported vary depending on the sources, the gap between groups is consistent. The average 4-year on-time graduation rate in the United States for all groups in recent years according to a study by the National Center for Education Statistics (Stetser & Stillwell, 2014) has been close to 81%; however, for blacks, American Indians, and Latinos it has been as low as 68%. For whites it was 85%, and for Asian/Pacific Islanders it was 93% (Stetser & Stillwell, 2014). As schools become more diverse, educators need new skills to reach students. What the research shows is that racial or ethnic differences in school performance can be reduced by focusing on student behavior and attitudes (Farrington et al., 2012).

In many schools, students and educators often come from different backgrounds. It takes less effort for educators to connect with students and parents who come from their same background including ethnic, racial, cultural, religious, or other identity. The findings are that most dropouts leave school because of bad experiences in school (Center for Public Education, 2010) and differences between school professionals and students can contribute to those experiences. Yet good conversations don't require both parties to have the same background. Reflective listening, honoring autonomy, and having an affirming attitude that recognizes strengths can help bridge differences. It is hard to be culturally insensitive if you are curious about students' lives and reflecting their thoughts and feelings rather than imposing your own perspective and your own solutions for them. MI can be a powerful tool for bridging cultural differences.

> *Good conversations don't require both parties to have the same background.*

MI conversations can engage students in conversations that draw out their cultural beliefs and connect them to what they value about school. A meta-analysis of MI in settings like addictions and health care showed double the effect size when offered to marginalized groups (blacks and Latinos) as compared to whites in changing behavior (Hettema et al., 2005). Put simply, MI provides a practical way to counter the powerlessness of marginalization.

MI Is Not the End-All

Admittedly, there is no single solution to the complex issues that contribute to the dropout problem. The research confirms that teacher–student relationships have a big impact on school completion (Center for Public Education, 2010) and MI is not unique in promoting that kind of relationship. But MI may well be an ideal way to begin, support, and maintain other efforts that increase students' sense of community, and maximize students' involvement in supporting engagement or intervention efforts. Your MI skills may help inspire students to take opportunities for optimal challenges that make learning interesting and ultimately increase staying in school, yet those opportunities need to be there. In the end, it's just one ingredient in what good schools have always done: maximize skill building and learning to prepare students to contribute to society by creating meaningful relationships and allowing students to develop and make decisions about who they are and what they want for their future so they can flourish as adults. (Box 15.2 provides an example of MI as an alternative to in-school suspension.)

Conclusion

The social and financial costs to society and to the individuals themselves of dropping out of school compels the field of education to find

---

BOX 15.2. MI as an Alternative to In-School Suspension (Chicago, 2006–2011)

Through a school–university partnership in Chicago, my colleagues and I (R. R.) initiated an innovative alternative to in-school suspension (ISS) at two large high schools. Instead of having students spend the day sitting in a room aimed at making boredom their punishment, they spent 1 day introduced to MI blended with experiential education. Sitting in a circle, the group was immediately drawn in with adventure-challenge initiatives that created laughter and built cooperation and trust. The MI-trained staff (and graduate students) then began individual MI conversations with the students. Since there were three times more students than providers, a third of the students were pulled out of the group for 35–40 minutes of individual MI at a time; the rest remained doing experiential activities that integrated debriefing conversations. This blended initiative was instantly engaging and surprised the students. The effort was conducted 1 day a week during the second semester for 5 years; on the other days of the week students went to the regular ISS. The dropout rates were examined the following semester, comparing participating students with those who attended the regular ISS. The results for participating students were 5–10% better retention—a small measure, yet the result of only one school day. We received comments from students like "This was the best day I've had in high school." Teachers noticed changes in attitude, attendance, and behavior.

effective strategies to improve student retention. Students who drop out are frequently the same ones with disruptive classroom behaviors. Helping these students change can create better outcomes for everyone. If MI can help move students from devaluing school to internalizing its importance, it can counter the peer culture of disengagement.

The need is clear, and having an additional tool available for intervening early, internalizing the value of learning, and creating a sense of community even in diverse schools, will improve their retention. Instead of rejecting the school or being rejected by the school, they will be more likely to engage in their schooling, all simply through conversations. When students see and internalize the value of school or to make a change that they own, decisions and a positive attitude and behavior will follow. Anyone who has a chance to have conversations with students will see that it is generally not hard to engage them in thinking about themselves and their future.

Transition to Life after School

Education is not the filling of a pail, but the
lighting of a fire.
—*William Butler Yeats*

When students graduate, a significant change is about to begin. With adequate fuel the change process can continue for quite some time. Educators' goal is to keep their students' fires burning.

Consider a student called Sofia, who is unable to decide what she wants to do. She excelled in math, something her teacher in sixth grade recognized when Sofia first arrived in the United States knowing only Spanish. She barely passed many other subjects as she worked on her language fluency. She could be the first in her family to go to college, but should she take that giant leap into a new world? She thinks, "Do I belong there? Will I be able to handle it?"

This chapter explores how MI can be used to address the multiple challenges faced by students as they make important decisions about their future after high school. Even short caring conversations can light a fire to help them weather the storms and remain committed to their goals.

The Challenge

Transition out of school often highlights ambivalence students feel about the changes ahead. The routes students choose will ideally prepare

them for jobs and careers, yet deciding which to take is often challenging. Students need to explore the
possibilities, create goals, and be
prepared for any hardships to get to
the right place.

> *Transition out of school
> often highlights ambivalence
> about the changes ahead.*

Demographic researchers suggest that by 2020 two out of three
jobs in the United States will require some college or other postsecondary education and by that year at the current rate there will be 5 million
too few college-educated individuals to meet workplace demands (Public Policy Institute, 2013). Similar workforce demands and changes
seem to be evolving elsewhere. Surveys in Europe also show the importance of university education to gainful employment (Schomburg &
Teichler, 2006). The pressure is on for effective guidance.

Unemployment due to lack of qualifications, along with the steady
deflation of pay for unskilled work over the past two decades, makes
postsecondary education almost a necessity to obtain a livable wage.
College graduates earn nearly twice as much as those with only high
school diplomas (Leonhardt, 2014). By helping students to transition
into postsecondary education and to think about their future careers,
teachers will prepare them for a better future.

Every year, many students finish high school uncertain what to
do next and unprepared for the challenges ahead. The push by schools
and parents for students to continue their studies and acquire skills is
showing mixed results. While growing numbers of students of all backgrounds are enrolling in colleges or other postsecondary schools, they
often lack follow-through and persistence. A majority of high school
graduates say they plan to enroll in college, but many never enroll and
others who enroll do not show up. Evidence suggests that personal
agency and college preparation including realistic expectations ("getting ready" behaviors) improve student persistence (Stage & Hossler,
2000; Attinasi, 1989; Braxton, 1995; Tinto & Wallace, 1986).

Increasingly, male students are not attending college at the same
rate as female students, 61% versus 71% (National Center for Education Statistics, 2014). There is also a higher college completion rate for
women, which is due to their superior academic performance (Buchmann & DiPrete, 2006). Yet we know that academic performance is
influenced by effort and is therefore changeable. The demographic distribution of who is going to college as well as who is completing college
shows that in the United States, African American and Latino students
often underperform, while whites are more likely to attend top-funded

institutions (Carnevale & Strohl, 2013). The result is a gap between various racial, ethnic, and gender groups in the percentages that enroll, attend, and persist.

A majority of students in many open-access colleges and postsecondary institutions attend for a time but do not persist to graduation (Carnevale & Strohl, 2013). It is likely that many had not anticipated the challenges or prepared themselves adequately for what they would face. Some blame it on academically unprepared students, while others claim that students just lack grit or resilience, the determination to do what it takes.

Studies suggest that inadequate academic preparedness is only partially to blame (Farrington et al., 2012). Researchers find that characteristics like persistence and motivation are critical, as are commitment and skills for managing time, planning, and organizing. Understanding that ability and intelligence are not fixed but rather something that can grow intentionally through effort and choice is how mastery occurs (Dweck, 2006; Farrington et al., 2012). A student's decision to put in this effort is crucial.

How students are treated and how they perceive adults' expectations of them can undermine (or bolster) determination and effort. It is not uncommon for minority groups to attest that they were made to feel inadequate, pushed into nonacademic fields, or told "You are not college material," regardless of their academic performance. Undoubtedly, the way educators interact with students as they decide and prepare for their future can make a difference. The process of thinking about the future is often done best in conversation with another person. Taking a nonjudgmental stance can prevent this marginalization while offering more autonomy.

How students perceive our expectations of them can undermine (or bolster) determination and effort.

The challenge for schools is to help each student to become fully aware, committed, and prepared for the educational journey ahead, regardless of the choices each makes.

How MI Can Help

Journeys can either be planned or spontaneous. For some students going to college is a given, an expectation internalized from parents, teachers, or mentors. For these students the decisions involve where to go or what to study. For others, particularly students from families without college in their background, the first decision is what to do. MI can be helpful in exploring options, making decisions, and strengthening commitment.

Preparatory conversations exploring students' interests, desires, abilities, and needs can be particularly valuable. They help students sort out preferences, often guided by their goals and values. MI can then be used to explore ambivalence about continued studies and hone in on change talk. It helps students process their thoughts and educators minimize any unintentional biases.

MI helps teachers and counselors become more mindful of how to guide conversations with students and thus avoid lowering expectations, undermining capabilities, or failing to recognize competence. The risk of prematurely suggesting what students should do will be avoided. This is particularly important with students who have doubts about exploring postsecondary options. MI helps prevent stereotyping of students from traditionally underrepresented groups that could push them away from what they are interested in pursuing.

> *MI helps us to avoid lowering expectations, undermining capabilities, or overlooking competence.*

As part of the push to go to college, MI conversations can help students to navigate the financial aid and college application processes. It can strengthen student motivation to show up and persist to graduation. Helping students consider things like financial and time constraints, interpersonal relationships, or any doubts they have before enrolling will make them better prepared. Because of this, MI has the potential to help students reach their educational or career goals and increase the likelihood that they will not only enroll in further education, but show up and persist until graduation.

MI conversations may be useful in the formation of student mindsets and attitudes for gaining skills, strategies, and readiness to persist or seek assistance when needed. For instance, these conversations can counter students' belief that their ability to succeed is fixed and unchangeable. Instead, MI can help students explore how their effort is and has been important and promote the development of a growth rather than a fixed mind-set (Dweck, 2006).

Neutrality

Almost all the conversations considered thus far had at least one thing in common—the school professional's intentions and actions were *not* neutral; the conversations had the goal of a particular change guided by the student's positive aspirations. For example, the student wanted to get along better with peers or to do better at academic subjects.

During many conversations about transition or careers, educators can be neutral. A teacher or counselor might want to consciously avoid influencing the student in any particular direction with a student who is selecting a career or college, choosing a subject to study, deciding whether to go to college right away, or considering a job with a relative. In these circumstances the conversation involves helping a student make a choice among equally valid options. Ambivalence is usually present, and attention is focused on letting the student explore this ambivalence and make decisions, without the gentle steering used in most MI conversations. This kind of "shared decision making" is also explored in more detail in Miller and Rollnick (2013).

Decisional Balance Exercise

A practical exercise governed by neutrality is called the "decisional balance." It's a tool for considering two options, one that gives equal conversational time to the pros and cons of each choice. The student considers the "good" things and the "bad" things of each option—for example, "In comparing the colleges you are considering, maybe we can explore what would be the advantages and disadvantages of you going to College X and then we can do the same for College Y." The pros and cons of going full time or part time or living at home or away from home can be useful to consider. It is worth mentioning that you should only use the decisional balance exercise with neutrality, that is, if you are *not* trying to encourage a particular change (Miller & Rose, 2015).

> *"Decisional balance" is an exercise governed by neutrality.*

Some students will find it helpful to write down their views so they can examine them thoughtfully (see Box 16.1). Others might find a simple conversation more helpful. Our experience has been that *how* the task is carried out is as important as what is done. This is where the supportive style and skills of MI provide a cocoon within which the student can face uncertainty with courage and clarity. How students feel about their options and their emotional safety is as important as more concrete things like where they might live or how to manage money.

BOX 16.1. Decisional Balance Example: Enrolling in College

	Option 1: Going full time	Option 2: Going part time
Pros	Good things about full time	Good things about part time
Cons	Bad things about full time	Bad things about part time

Personal Values Card Sort

Decisions about transitions provide an invaluable opportunity for students to decide what's really important to them. The personal values card sort is an exercise in which students sort through, rate, and select cards that best describe their personal values. These then serve as a foundation for making decisions about their educational goals and careers. As with the decisional balance exercise described above, the task is simple and sequential. However, it's in the execution—the use of core skills in a supportive atmosphere—that students can come to a new sense of who they are and where they might go in life. It is an opportunity students will appreciate if they are adequately engaged beforehand.

How the task is carried out is as important as what the task is.

Box 16.2 provides instructions for how to carry out the card sort. These instructions, and the values on the cards, can be adapted to suit the age and needs of the student and the time available. A print-ready copy of the cards and a detailed description of the use of this tool can be found at *www.motivationalinterviewing.org* (under "Resources"). You may choose to reduce the number of cards to focus on topics most likely to influence career decision making. You will want to provide some blank cards for students to add values that are not included.

A short version of the personal values card sort was used to help a student explore whether or not she wanted to go to college. When she was asked to select her top five values, she picked mastery, challenge, commitment, independence, and genuineness. What follows is a part of the MI conversation that then took place.

TEACHER: I wonder if you would share what "mastery" means to you?

STUDENT: I value being good at doing things and also understanding

BOX 16.2. Personal Values Card Sort
(Miller, C'de Baca, Matthews, & Wilbourne, 2001)

Put together a set of cards that each list a value pertinent to the students' education and career choices (see also *www.motivationalinterviewing.org* under "Resources"). Also create three "rating cards" (see below).

1. Ask the students to "place each card under one of the three rating cards: 'very important to me'; 'important to me'; or 'not important to me.' You may put up to eight cards in the 'very important' category." Let students know they can write values on blank cards if the values they want are not included. Explain that after they are finished with this part, there will be one more task. Allow enough time for this rating.

2. Explain the second task: "Now, focus on your 'very important' values cards and sort them with the card you value the most on top, second most next, and so on. Do you have any questions?"

3. Use these values to help the students think about the decisions they are making regarding their postsecondary lives, using OARS.

things. I want to feel like I'm an expert. Like I'm good at math and I like the feeling I get from it. I'm interested in getting good at other things. Like I'm starting to learn how to play the piano from my aunt and I'd like to get good at it. [Change talk]

TEACHER: You're a person that is interested in getting good at the things you are interested in. Also, from the next cards, it seems like you're willing to take on difficult tasks and you're not one to give up easily. [Reflection and affirmation]

STUDENT: I guess you could say that (*smile*). I've always liked challenges, like math problems that seem difficult for others. I think music is similar and I'd like to get good at reading music and playing it.

TEACHER: Your inquisitive mind is one that is willing to take on new challenges and learning to read music and play the piano is something that you've recently taken on. [Reflection and affirmation]

STUDENT: Yes and I also like to be independent. I'm tired of being told what to do all the time.

TEACHER: As you look at the values you picked, including

independence, how might they help you make choices about your future, college for instance? [Open question]

STUDENT: Well, I think college will help me get good at certain things and be challenged. It would also let me be more independent since I could leave home. [Change talk] I'm not sure how well I will do there since I've heard there are lots of writing requirements and I am not that good at writing. I'm also worried about how much it will cost since my parents can't help much.

TEACHER: You have some concerns about writing and you want to make sure you figure out how you to deal with that as well as how to pay for college. You like the idea of being an expert in things you decide on, like math or even music. [Reflection]

STUDENT: Yeah, I've mentioned the idea to my parents and they also are worried about how much it will cost. I also think they are worried about me being away from home. But, to be honest, that idea sounds exciting.

TEACHER: You're starting to see yourself as a college student and one of the barriers you see is paying for it. I wonder what you want to do to explore this and if there are other barriers that might be good to anticipate?

STUDENT: I'm planning to meet with the postsecondary coach to do my student aid application and I heard on a field trip to a campus about having tutors available. So, I'm thinking it probably will be OK since I could get help with writing. I'm not one to give up easily. [Change talk]

TEACHER: Wow, you're starting to sound like a success story before you start! What's your next step? [Affirmation and open question]

STUDENT: I guess I need to have a heart-to-heart talk with my parents and see where that takes me. I feel like they want me to stay home and go to a local college. I really want to leave.

TEACHER: Being genuine or honest is another value you hold and that goes with the way you deal with your parents. I'm happy to help you and even your parents explore your options if you want, whatever you decide to do. So, if you want to keep me posted that will be great.

STUDENT: This is helpful. Sure, I'll tell you what happens with my parents.

TEACHER: Let's catch up soon; take care.

Conclusion

MI has the potential to help students transition to life after high school. It can be an effective ingredient in conversations about attending postsecondary education, potentially helping to equalize the gap between groups going on to postsecondary education related to background, class, culture, race, or gender. For students becoming the first generation in their families to go to college, it can help them anticipate the barriers and prepare for the challenges. It can be a valuable means for supporting student exploration of careers or other crucial postsecondary decisions.

Professionally it can help educators minimize biases or stereotypes and become more careful in guiding conversations in ways that minimize their influence, yet help students in the decision-making process so they own their decisions. Strengthened commitment and determination will likely be the result. The fire within them will be strong enough to keep burning.

BROADER HORIZONS

Now that you have a grasp of what MI is and how it can help you to get the most out of your everyday conversations with your students, consider what it may take to learn these skills deeply. Part IV steps away from the classrooms and corridors to addresses two topics: (1) how to practice and develop your MI skills; and (2) how you might integrate MI in your schools. We present several models developed by others to use MI to help students overcome a variety of challenges, while also considering the organizational changes in your setting that may contribute to the success of implementing MI.

17

Improving Your
Knowledge and Skills

The harder I practice, the luckier I get.
                                    —*Gary Player*

How do you learn MI? One answer is obvious: you have already begun, in the countless hours you spend trying to help students to improve. You talk about this or that change, observe, discuss, and talk some more. Many of the core skills are widely used in everyday life. MI merely sharpens your use of them and your awareness of what you say and why.

What is not in this chapter is probably the best learning tool of all: your students. You could think of their reactions to how you speak as real-time feedback about your engagement with them, how open they are to change, and what barriers may exist for them. You can use this feedback to improve your flexibility in responding to them. It's in these moments, when you notice the impact of a shift in your approach, that some of the fastest progress in skill development takes place. The ideal learning outcome for this chapter is that it stimulates you to step out and be bold, modify your style, steer the conversation gently, listen harder, observe your own progress, and practice some more.

This chapter is designed mainly for use on your own and goes through selected topics in a sequence that roughly follows the order of chapters in Part I, starting with the broad attitudes and the style that serve as the foundation for MI. It then moves through some of the skills and practice challenges. You will notice that it covers:

- Some additional knowledge that extends the content of Part I.
- Exercises you can do right now.

This chapter has an older sister, a comprehensive guide to the skillful practice of MI, which contains a large number of exercises and associated explanations: this is *Building MI Skills* by David Rosengren (2009). It served as the inspiration for this chapter and is highly recommended reading.

Whom Would You Like to Speak with?

MI has gained traction in many settings because practitioners have noticed that negative judgments about someone's motivation typically leads to unhelpful conversation and poor outcomes. These interactions are often easier said than done: you look to hold back from questioning someone's motivation, give them space to face the future, offer them affirmation and respect, and their motivation often grows in front of you. That's MI in a nutshell. It's fundamentally strengths-based.

Doing MI well is not solely a technical matter of using this or that skill, like affirmation or complex reflection, but of minding your background attitude and judgments. It can be like putting on a different pair of spectacles, a metaphor that served as the inspiration for the exercise that follows.

Try This

This is a trick of the imagination, so be warned. Suppose that a *colleague asks you to do her a favor: to help two students improve their progress.* Which of them would you prefer to see?

Student 1

Kurt has been late for school almost every day for 2 weeks, and when he comes in he thinks he owns the place and doesn't even lift his head to acknowledge anyone else. Kurt's grades are so poor that it will soon be time for quite drastic remedial action. Then there's the fact that his social skills are poor, and he can be rude to teachers if pressed for an answer to something. Last week he hit another student and was suspended for 3 days and had to bring a parent into school to talk about it all.

How do you feel about this young man about to enter your room? What if you were to see three students like Kurt in a row? Most people would say not very happy, and some would have contrasting urges to either lay down the law or try to avoid doing this colleague a favor in the future. Now consider this student:

Student 2

Jim lives with his older brother, although his grandmother is about to take him in. His dad has never been around, and his mother died last year. He washes his own clothes and prepares meals for himself and his brother when he returns from work. He finds it hard to get up in the morning because he uses the Internet quite late each night, so he gets to school late. He doesn't feel very optimistic, doesn't do as well as he would like to in school, and lost his temper recently when a younger boy teased and threatened him.

How would you feel about seeing Jim? Probably a mixture of concern, admiration, and perhaps some weariness about where to start.

The point here will be obvious by now: they are the same student. The first account was colored by the lens of "deficit thinking" (Corbett, 2009) and judgments about poor motivation, the second judged by one biased in favor of Jim's strengths. Adopting the latter perspective does not mean you would not address his poor performance or behavioral difficulties, let alone condone them. But it simply entails viewing Jim as a competent human being, giving you a platform for a better conversation. You will feel better, and so will Jim. It's easier to judge people than not to. MI involves a clear steer toward positive judgments and away from negative ones.

Viewing a student as a competent human being gives you a platform for a better conversation.

Practice the Spirit of MI

If you think of a student as a thorn in your side, or riddled with nothing but problems, it becomes difficult to even conceive of how you might use MI. What we called the spirit is about two things (see Chapter 3): how to establish a helpful empathic relationship and how to gently steer the conversation in a productive direction, what we called evoking. This rather abstract account of the mind-set and heart-set of MI might seem inaccessible to learning, and indeed, a common question raised, for example, is can you learn to empathize? Yet without a facility for these things, there is no MI, only dance steps without the dance, or notes without a melody.

Try This

Empathy: The Key to Acceptance, Compassion, and Partnership

If there is a clear route to grasping and actually demonstrating to students that you are accepting, compassionate, and collaborative, it is probably through the single idea of experiencing and demonstrating empathy, the ability to stand in another's shoes. Actually, that's two processes. The first sits inside you, having the experience, while the second involves what you say and how you say it. Once you experience empathy, the use of reflective listening and affirmation provide the key to helping students feel that you understand them *without judgment,* that you accept them as human beings, and that you are willing to work with them in partnership. Core skills like reflection and affirmation have been illustrated throughout this book. The three brief exercises below therefore focus on the experience of empathy itself. Curiosity seems to be a key.

1. Watch one of these empathy clips:
   - Knowledge Center
     (*www.youtube.com/watch?v=AZ-pU7ozt3g*)
   - Cleveland Clinic
     (*www.youtube.com/watch?v=cDDWvj_q-o8*)

One of these clips starts with a quotation from Thoreau—"Could a greater miracle take place than for us to look through each other's eyes for an instant?"—the other from Steinbeck—"You only understand people if you feel them in yourself." They are followed by a simple presentation of images with words alongside to describe peoples' experiences. It is designed to elicit empathy, and end with a striking question.

How this simple observation exercise applies to school life is obvious. Indeed, does it raise the possibility of school projects in which students themselves make such a collection? Empathy is essentially about improving relationships. It works both ways. It also furthers a student's emotional and social development.

2. Watch a movie or a TV show and turn down the sound, or watch one in a language you do not understand. Try to tell the feelings being expressed, paying attention to nonverbal cues. Just let your

mind try to interpret their facial expressions, movements, gestures, and posture to be able to interpret their feelings and thoughts. After a few exchanges, if it is in English, you can turn back on the volume or, if not in English, the subtitles. See how accurate you were.

3. Discretely people-watch in a public setting. This might involve looking at your students in the cafeteria, at an airport, a train station, or a restaurant and trying to interpret the emotions that they seem to have as they communicate with others. And if you are close enough for eavesdropping, even though it is frowned upon, it is commonplace and useful in increasing your empathy muscle. What would it be like to be that person?

Evoking

This remains the defining heart of MI that complements the experience and practice of empathy: looking forward in a conversation with a genuine sense of curiosity as you steer things so that the student develops a new sense of how change might come about. We have noticed that we do this well when we are very restrained, even in the briefest conversations, and hold back from judgment or trying to solve the challenge for the student.

Imagine you are a tourist unable to speak the language and you were wishing you had a guide next to you as you encountered the following situations:

1. What thoughts and feelings would you want this guide to know about you in each of the following situations?

Situation	Thoughts	Feelings
In a café, but uncertain what to eat		
Exhausted on a hike, but like the exercise		
Need rest, yet want to see cultural events		
Enjoying it, yet homesick		

2. Now pretend to be that guide and use statements (not questions) to find out. Each statement should begin with "You."

3. What state of mind did you need to have as the guide to come up with those statements?

MI Spirit in Action

As we've outlined, the elements of the MI spirit are both experiences within you, such as your thoughts about your students' strengths and your sense of how they feel about change, as well as ways of bringing the internal experiences outward in a supportive way, for your students to experience as they consider change. Here is a quick and simple worksheet that you can adapt however you see fit. It invites you to reflect on your conversations with your students, the ways you've brought elements of partnership, acceptance, compassion, and evocation to life.

Situation (setting, student, change being considered . . .)	How was I consistent with the MI spirit?	If applicable, how could I have been more consistent with the MI spirit?
Partnership (collaborative style; a conversation between "two experts")		
Acceptance (nonjudgmentally acknowledging a student's choice)		
Compassion (acting in student's best interests based on *his or her own* goals/ values)		
Evocation (drawing out what the student thinks/feels about all aspects of a change he or she is considering)		

Can You Tame the Righting Reflex?

Simple challenges with an engaged student can respond well to instruction. However, there's a difference between consciously deciding to instruct or correct a student, on the one hand, and using the "righting reflex" (see Chapters 1 and 8), on the other. The former can be thoughtful, well timed, and effective, promoting autonomy and competence, while the latter looks and feels different. It's a less-conscious, almost automatic response to a problem in which you see a student struggling and simply tell him or her why or how to change. The more complex the problem, the more troublesome the outcome might be.

Self-awareness is probably the first step to taming the righting reflex, and one's emotional state, positive or negative, is what usually lights the fire underneath its use. It's harder to be patient, to listen, and to help someone to solve a problem for him- or herself when your emotional state is ramped up.

Then there are quieter times when a conversation is going fine, and the impulse to use the righting reflex strikes. It's often in the middle of a conversation. When you notice this urge, it might make sense to shift gears and adopt the guiding style that's more consistent with MI. *It's hard to listen when your emotional state is ramped up.* Often the use of a reflection in these moments recalibrates the conversation in a more collaborative way. Sharpening your ability to recognize patterns of conversation that go well and not so well will save you time and energy.

Try This

This exercise gives you a chance to stop, think, and consider an alternative to the righting reflex. For each of the two scenarios below, we also provide our own alternatives to the righting reflex. For your part, simply write down an alternative to the righting reflex as well as the student's anticipated response to your idea.

Scenario 1: High stakes, calming response needed

STUDENT: If I hear that again I'm going to hit her, she's so pathetic.

ADMINISTRATOR: I'm sorry but if you do that you could be in big trouble, OK? [Using the righting reflex]

STUDENT: Well, what do you expect me to do? You all make me sick.

Is there some way you can avoid the righting reflex, and calm the situation down?

STUDENT: If I hear that again I'm going to hit her, she's so pathetic.

Your response (avoiding the righting reflex): _____

_____

_____

Student: _____

_____

_____

Anything you say to come alongside an upset student, and show him or her that you grasp what he or she feels, will help, especially if you give him or her choices. Here's one possible response:

STUDENT: If I hear that again I'm going to hit her, she's so pathetic.

ADMINISTRATOR: It sounds like you are feeling really upset. Would you like to have a quiet chat or are you going to be OK?

STUDENT: I don't know what to do, she just drives me crazy because . . . (calming down and telling the story).

Scenario 2: Everyday learning challenge

STUDENT: Sorry, but I just forgot my book at home and it's like crazy there in the morning.

TEACHER: Well, that's not acceptable. You must try to be more organized. [Using the righting reflex]

STUDENT: I am organized, but it's too rushed at home; it's not my fault.

Is there a way you can avoid telling the student what he probably already knows? Does it really help him change his behavior to "hammer home" this message? His defensive reaction above does not sound like a student who is learning and open to change. See what alternative you can come up with.

STUDENT: Sorry, but I just forgot my book at home and it's like crazy there in the morning.

Your response (avoiding the righting reflex): _____

_____

_____

Student: _____

_____

_____

If the student understands the need to change, what can you do instead of using the righting reflex? Using a guiding style might be an alternative, illustrated here:

STUDENT: Sorry, but I just forgot my book at home and it's like crazy there in the morning.

TEACHER: What's going to help you remember, I wonder?

STUDENT: I don't know. Maybe . . . (*giving it some thought*).

In small moments like those above when alternatives to the righting reflex open up, you will often notice change talk emerging in response.

Open Questions That Open Windows (the "O" in "OARS")

Open questions (see Chapter 5) are like saying to a student, "I think we might consider this and I'm quite interested to hear what your thoughts are. . . . " Put simply, they allow the student space to speak freely with less chance of falling into a question–answer trap. The other core skills are there to give you the freedom to get the best out of an open question. So choose it wisely, and sit back.

Try This

Here's a 10-item quiz. The task is to identify which of the four processes the following open questions are asked in the service of. Your choice is therefore to place engaging (E), focusing (F), evoking (Ev), or planning (P) alongside each one. If you get confused, conduct a quick scan of Chapter 4 to clarify the differences between the processes. We've provided our answers below. Notice how we tried to form the questions to be as short and as simple as possible. A quick rule of thumb would be that the purpose of engaging is to come alongside and understand; focusing to establish direction in the conversation; evoking to bring out the student's views about change; and planning to encourage the student to say specifically how that might come about.

1. What do you think might change? _____
2. What exactly happened? _____
3. What would be most helpful for us to talk about? _____
4. Why do you feel so angry? _____
5. How might you actually do that from now on? _____
6. Why might you want to find different friends? _____
7. What would you most like to work on today? _____
8. What's the next step that will really make a difference? _____
9. What sort of changes make sense to you? _____
10. What sort of grades would you really like to get? _____

Our judgments were that questions 2 and 4 would help with engaging; questions 3 and 7 with focusing; questions 1, 6, 9, and 10 with evoking; and questions 5 and 8 with planning.

Affirm, Even in the Face of Failure (the "A" in "OARS")

A skill like affirmation (see Chapter 5) cannot exist in isolation from an effort to engage, be genuine, and be helpful. Otherwise its use can descend into a caricature of the real thing, for example, that it's just about "being nice" to a student. That's a distortion of something that is much more than that, with the potential to transform a student. It can be useful to ask yourself what the difference is between praise and affirmation. Here are examples:

"Well done. I'm impressed with your work today." [praise]
"You've been determined to get the job done today." [affirmation]

To appreciate the difference, imagine being at the receiving end of each one of these statements. Put simply, in the first the student is being rewarded with the teacher's approval; in the second the teacher highlights a positive quality *within* the student, a quality that is likely enduring. While praise has its place in child rearing and education, its dependence on extrinsic motivation is a fragile thing, none more so than when a student fails, and the sense of shame that may emerge in anticipation of disapproval or even punishment. A better balance in favor of using affirmation more than praise will reap rewards as the student takes ownership of his or her progress.

The more complex the challenge facing a student, the more useful affirmation might be. Consider what happens in the light of failure. The inclination in judging the situation is to point out where the weakness lies, tell the student how to fix things ("No, that's not right; the answer is B not A; you're not thinking clearly enough"), or if it's a behavioral issue, to pass judgment, point to better behavior, or even issue punishment if its serious enough. Instead, what might the impact of affirmation be in these circumstances, to use their strengths as the platform for improvement?

> *The more complex the challenge facing a student, the more useful affirmation might be.*

Try This

See if you can formulate an affirmation in the face of difficulty, and also anticipate the student's reply. Here is an example:

STUDENT: I've messed up here, right here.

TEACHER'S AFFIRMATION: You tried hard, and you can see where this has gone wrong.

STUDENT'S REPLY: Yes, I did try, and I want to get this right.

Exercise 1

STUDENT: I'm frustrated. This is the fourth time I've tried solving this equation and it's still wrong!

Your affirmation: _____

_____

_____

Student's reply: _____

_____

_____

Our suggestion: You are determined to get this right.

Exercise 2

STUDENT: Just because something helps others doesn't mean that it will work for me!

Your affirmation: _____

_____

_____

Student's reply: _____

_____

_____

Our suggestion: You know your own mind and what's going to work for you.

Exercise 3

Affirmation can focused on a wide range of things, including a student's effort, skills, positive personality traits, beliefs, or goals. There is no right affirmation, yet it takes being observant and mindful to produce them. In Box 17.1 we list some student characteristics and provide an affirmation for each. Can you provide a second example? You may want to start with words like "You value . . . "; "You're really good at . . . "; "You're a person who . . . "; "You care about . . . "; "You're so . . . "; or "That must make you feel. . . ."

Forming Reflections (the "R" in "OARS")

Many adults, particularly those who have come to rely on asking questions as the vehicle for communication, struggle to form and use reflective listening statements (see Chapter 5). Thankfully, we've found that many individuals have the capacity to learn to use reflections, such as young adults or even quite young children, many of whom are able to clear their minds of distracting thoughts and simply be curious, the essential starting point. The essence of reflection is curiosity expressed in a statement, not a question. If, after doing the following exercise, you practice the skill in everyday life, and consciously form a dozen reflections for a couple of days, you would be well on top of most of what it takes to use MI at school.

Practice this every day and it will be much easier to learn MI.

BOX 17.1 Form Your Own Affirmation

Student characteristic	Affirmation
Student is always loud, sometimes aggressive.	1. You are an enthusiastic person. 2. _____
Student never misses class, keeps trying when frustrated with challenging material.	1. Your commitment shows in many ways. 2. _____
Student makes and sells her paintings to help her family financially.	1. Wow, as young as you are and you're so entrepreneurial. 2. _____
Student is social, loves attention, and is very influential with her peers.	1. You're a natural leader. 2. _____
Student is interested in sports which is what makes his schooling important.	1. You're a serious athlete; you love it. 2. _____
Student is shy, quiet, and when she talks it shows sincerity.	1. You're a thoughtful person. 2. _____
Student usually goes through a crisis with a sense of humor.	1. Your positive energy brightens everyone up. 2. _____

Try This

Reflective listening involves forming a hypothesis about what someone is saying, meaning, or feeling. This simple exercise is adapted from Rosengren's (2009) workbook on learning MI, mentioned above. Here are three different student statements. We provide one reflection for each and your task is to form the other two.

STUDENT: I seem to get into fights for no reason.

Our reflection: You mean that you don't plan to have a fight.

You mean that (your reflection) _____

_____

_____

You mean that (your reflection) _____

_____

_____

STUDENT: I hate math.

Our reflection: You mean that math is not your *favorite* subject.

You mean that (your reflection) _____

_____

_____

You mean that (your reflection) _____

_____

_____

STUDENT: I want to be a train driver.

Our reflection: You mean that that would be really exciting.

You mean that (your reflection) _____

_____

_____

You mean that (your reflection) _____

_____

_____

With each reflection of yours, the students will continue speaking, expanding on how they are feeling because they sense your desire to understand and connect. You'll notice that different reflections of a single statement lead the students in slightly different directions.

Summary of What? (the "S" in "OARS")

A summary is a crossroad in a conversation where confusion can be clarified, engagement enhanced, resolve to change solidified, and a new direction forged (see Chapter 5). There's quite a lot of choice, so what do you summarize? To a large degree, it depends on what you want. In MI, we want to help the student to face change.

Try This

Consider the following three summaries *of the same conversation* with a student in a conversation about life in school. They are all quite short, simple, and easy to deliver. About what are they?

Summary 1

"Your grades have been poor this year, you can do better, and last week you got into trouble with being late, and instead of taking your punishment in that extra class, you got cross and behaved badly. You know you have done that, and now you are sitting down with me to hear about the next step."

Summary 2

"You feel that it wasn't your fault that you were so late and that your grades have suffered, and that you behaved badly when you got cross because that other student started pushing you and you lost your temper."

Summary 3

"You feel some of this has been unfair. You are a determined guy, and this sometimes gets you into trouble. You would like to avoid losing your temper in the future. You are concerned about your grades, and also don't mind looking for ways of getting to class on time."

Study these three summaries and answer the following two questions *before* looking at our reflections that follow:

1. Which one is most consistent with MI and why?
2. What will the reaction of the student be to each one and why?

Most Consistent with MI?

It's the third summary because there is a focus on student strengths, with an affirmation like "You are a determined guy," but most importantly a focus on the future and what the student said about change,

MI is forward looking with a keen eye on the student's own reasons to change.

what we have called change talk. MI is forward looking with a very keen eye on the student's own good reasons to change.

The second summary, while it might have been perfectly accurate, only focused on deficits and problems. The first one is obviously not consistent with MI; indeed, it's effectively the polar opposite of it.

Reaction of the Student?

The first summary might capture the challenges, but it is delivered in such a punitive and judgmental manner that is bound to leave the student feeling downhearted, if not scared and demoralized. The effect upon change is for you to reflect upon. Our guess is that it's the kind of summary that closes the window of change for most students.

The second summary could certainly improve engagement and leave the student feeling understood. But what next might happen is not clear. The third summary should leave the student feeling engaged, and might help to encourage change, especially if it is followed up with further conversation.

Change Talk: Harnessing Strengths

Chapter 6 highlighted what change talk is, and how you might notice it, elicit more, and respond to it constructively. This can get quite technical, like becoming aware of the strength of change talk, and different forms it can take. Yet the overriding requirement at the heart of MI is something quite simple: to work with a student's strengths and aspirations, to search for his or her positive qualities, even when what he or she says so often seems to be about problems and reasons why he or she won't or can't change. That's as much an attitude and state of mind as it is a technical task. The exercise below is designed to challenge you to notice these qualities, with one restriction: respond with a reflection or affirmation only. You'll notice the student getting stronger. Our suggestions sit beneath each scenario.

Try This

Answer the questions for each scenario below, including a reflection that might evoke more change talk. Our suggestions are placed at the end.

Scenario 1

A student talks about homework: "I tell you, it's a struggle getting to homework for me, whatever you might say. I'd like to, but I get home and my brothers are partying and fighting and I can't find space to sit down and think. Then we must make food and it's eat, more partying, and sleep. And then I get into trouble at school, so what's new?"

1. What strengths and aspirations might lie beneath this student's statement? Provide two to three possibilities.

_____

_____

_____

2. How might you respond with a reflection? Provide two to three possibilities.

_____

_____

_____

Scenario 2

A student talks about friends: "She's my best friend 1 minute then she comes over all horrible and there's trouble. So I try to make things better and then some of the others take her side. So I just walk away sometimes and tell myself to keep my cool. I just feel like I can't trust her and maybe I should drop our friendship because I can't focus on my classes."

1. What strengths and aspirations might lie beneath this student's statement? Provide two to three possibilities.

_____

_____

_____

2. How might you respond with a reflection? Provide two to three possibilities.

_____

_____

_____

Our Suggestions

The student in Scenario 1 would like things to be different, and indeed said that she'd like to do more homework (change talk). She says she "struggles," which suggest that she might be quite determined sometimes, and her reference to making food suggests that she also takes responsibility for feeding others. Among the reflections we thought of were, "You have to use a lot of your determination to overcome these challenges"; "If you could overcome these obstacles, you might succeed in getting more homework done"; "You'd like to get more homework done if you could"; or "At home the lack of a peaceful place makes it difficult for you to do homework, yet you're a person that has overcome challenges to do better for yourself."

The student in Scenario 2 shows maturity, recognizing that focusing on being upset is interfering with her school performance and that trustworthiness and keeping her cool is key to good friendships. Interpersonal threats can distract and undermine learning, as seen in this example, and, petty as it may seem, helping her process what happens next is important. You may want to reflect and affirm by acknowledging her insight and maturity in dealing with her feelings as she decides what to do. You may want to provide a reflection that affirms her strengths and the contrast, in tune with what she mentioned: "You're a trustworthy person and wish your best friend would be the same toward you" or "You prize loyalty and friendship and wish your friends would have equally honorable characteristics." You could also reflect by highlighting a noble character trait: "You are someone who can keep your cool even when you feel disrespected" or "Above all, you want to make sure your friendships don't interfere with your school performance."

Championing Autonomy in Tricky Situations

Freedom to make up one's own mind is a theme that runs through this book, many others, and bodies of theory and research; some would even say it is fundamental to student learning and change. We certainly notice this in the conduct of conversations about change. Here's where there might be room to become more skillful, and the aim of the exercises to follow. Even in some tough situations, where you need to give a student advice, one can enhance autonomy at the same time (see Chapter 8).

What exactly hinders or promotes autonomy *in the way you speak to students?* We've noticed a number of things that do this. See if you can spot them.

Try This

The following teacher statements are ordered from low- to high-auton-omy promotion in the face of a difficult conversation to come. They could also quite easily be statements directed to a teacher, by his or her superior. Indeed, to get the best effect, imagine this latter scenario. You walk into your superior's office. What is it about all but the first state-ment that progressively enhances autonomy? With each statement there is something new added that does this even more than the previous one. What is it? How do they make you feel?

1. "I want to sit down with you now and look at the situation."
2. "I want to sit down with you now and see what you think about the situation."
3. "I want to sit down with you now and see what you think about the situation. Would that be OK with you?"
4. "I want to sit down with you now and see where you feel there might be room to improve the situation. Would that be OK with you?"
5. "I want to sit down with you now and see where you feel there might be room to improve the situation. I want to trust your judgment here. Would that be OK with you?"

These statements share things in common: read in isolation, they all sound quite normal and common; and they all affect autonomy, and your reaction, in various ways. The person making them wants to help solve a problem. The receiver, whether school professional or student, is going to immediately size up what he or she is "up against" and respond accordingly. How comfortably, and with what confidence of success, is a question worth asking. Our assumption is that this gets better as you go down the list, primarily because autonomy is being enhanced via the respect shown for the person and his or her choices.

Small things matter, or, put another way, nuances of language that convey your attitude and approach to change are easy for the person to pick up. In the above list we pinpointed quite a few of them:

• *Attending to power differentials.* Feeling less powerful than the person who is speaking to you evokes at least uncertainty, if not an ele-ment of helplessness in the face of the conversation to come. That first statement was fairly neutral. It carried a quiet indication of authority that could easily have been accentuated, for example, "I need to sit you down and look at the situation." No question about who has autonomy with that statement.

- *"Your perspective matters."* That's the essence of the second statement, and it's at the heart of MI. It generates comfort and a feeling of autonomy.

- *Permission.* The third statement includes this element. It needs to be genuine to enhance autonomy. When there is no choice possible, it is important to explain the rationale and acknowledge the person's feelings in return. An example: "It's required because it was decided it's best for students and I recognize that lack of choice can elicit a reaction."

- *Understated language.* One word, "might," signals the skillfulness of the fourth statement, and it enhances autonomy in an unobtrusive way like no other. Much of the language used in MI contains this modest quality, often contained in the wording of reflective listening statements.

- *Direct statements that champion autonomy.* The last statement enhances autonomy directly with "I want to trust your judgment here." Other examples include "It's up to you," "You'll be a good judge of what's best for you," and so on.

Our call here, and throughout this book, is to notice the effect on both you and the student of using language that promotes autonomy, and head out and practice. It should make for more satisfying conversations and probably more effective ones too.

With Colleagues: Two Short Exercises

Learning is often best done in small groups. We close this chapter with two exercises that you can practice in small groups. They address both the spirit and practice of MI.

Exercise 1: The Closed Fist[1]

This is one way of actually experiencing pressure to change. Have colleagues pair up and decide who will be #1 and #2. Ask the #1's to close one of their fists. Remind them that it is *their* fist and that they have

---

[1]Thanks to MINT members Alexander Kantchelov, Rik Bes, and Colleen Marshall for sharing this activity.

the right to do with it what they want, other than punch their partner. Tell #2's that their task is to get #1's to open their fist with no bribing or physical contact, only through conversation. Give them a minute or two.

Now ask questions like "What worked well?"; "What didn't work?"; and "How did you feel [on both sides of the experiment]?" People will readily talk about their freedom of choice (autonomy) and about what conditions favored change. How to use words to promote change is what MI seeks effective answers to.

Exercise 2: MI in a Nutshell[2]

If colleagues are willing to dive in and share their own experiences, much can be learned about how to encourage change. The exercise uses this starting point: "Something in my life I could change, but I am not sure about it." You simply ask colleagues to work in pairs, with one person prepared to talk about this possible change, the other trying to promote change. It's best to remind people *not* to choose something too personal, but to tackle a safe topic from their everyday life, perhaps connected to their lifestyle (e.g., exercise, diet) or a dilemma at work or home that is easy to talk about. The exercise can be enhanced by having a facilitator to direct practice and discussion.

Trial 1

As soon as the person tells you what he or she is considering changing, do the following (any order, repeat, continue until told to stop):

1. Ordering, directing, or commanding
2. Warning or threatening
3. Giving advice, making suggestions, or providing solutions
4. Persuading with logic, arguing, or lecturing
5. Moralizing, preaching, or telling the client what he or she "should" do
6. Disagreeing, judging, criticizing, or blaming

After this trial, allow those getting the help to share how helpful the conversation has been. Ask for adjectives that describe it, and, if you want, a number between 1 and 5 with their hands in the air on how helpful it was; one finger would mean "very unhelpful" and five fingers

---

[2]Thanks to Dr. William R. Miller for sharing this activity.

"very helpful"; scores could thus range from 1 to 5. You could even add the numbers together and compare outcomes after the next trial.

Trial 2

Ask the following questions; allow your partner to answer. Give him or her your full attention. Remember what he or she said so you can summarize "Why your partner is prepared to change" (#5).

1. "Why would you want to . . . [what your partner said he or she was considering changing]?"
2. "If you did decide, how would you do it?"
3. "What reasons are there . . . [to make that change]?"
4. "On a scale of 1 to 10, how important is it to you? Why?"
5. "It seems like you are prepared to change because . . . [give a summary of what you heard, why he or she is prepared to change]."
6. "What do you think you need to do to accomplish this?"

Allow the group to share their thoughts about what the difference between the two trials was and which they preferred. Ask for adjectives and add the number given on helpfulness (1–5) to compare. At the end of the discussion, explain that Trial 1 is based on some of the "barriers to communication" listed by Thomas Gordon in his "teacher effectiveness training" and Trial 2 is based on William Miller's "taste of MI" activity. This activity was developed by Miller and can be powerful as the first part of an introductory presentation.

The Next Step

Learning MI is often a personal journey, not unlike learning a new language, characterized by new ways of listening, asking questions, and developing ways to express empathy, which help students consider how they want their lives to unfold. You've already taken a step in your journey by reading this book. Whether this is your first exposure to MI or not, you've likely come to appreciate the importance of practice as you have with other skills you've developed. There are many ways to practice MI and the activities we present are but a sample of exercises that you can do by yourself, with another person, or in small groups. Should you wish to explore other ways of learning MI, you can find additional ideas at *www.motivationalinterviewing.org.*

Integrating MI in Schools

A journey of a thousand miles begins with
a single step.
                                        —*Lao Tse*

In order to get the most out of your investment of time in learning MI, it would help if your work setting supported the goals of MI, and if your colleagues worked in concert. You can't change an organization on your own, of course, but there are a number of things people have tried that have worked to create environments where MI can be potent, and can take hold for the long term. This chapter offers readers some ideas about choices educators can consider before integrating MI into their schools. A number of the strategies described below were the subject of research efforts that had MI focused on students' needs.

Who Does What?

School officials have several options when deciding how best to meet students' needs through the use of an MI-based program. Before embarking on any particular approach to integrating MI, educators need to consider several questions, including:

- Is it teachers and school staff who are the MI providers, or are they counselors from outside agencies?

- If these providers are from within the school, are these individual school staff members applying MI in their own settings, or is it a programwide or schoolwide effort?
- Are the MI providers other students, perhaps, trained in MI, and involved in a peer-led effort to help fellow students?
- Are the students involved (those receiving MI) considering changes directly linked to the school's mission (e.g., academic or classroom behavior), or are they considering a change outside the explicit mission of the school (e.g., drug use) that would nonetheless influence students' school performance?
- Is the focus not a specific problem, but an effort to use a strengths-based approach to create a more positive school climate?

What follows here is a list of specific strategies for weaving MI into the workings of a school. Depending on how you answered the questions above, one or more of these strategies may be a more appropriate choice than others. We do not present them in a range from less desirable models to more desirable ones. While we certainly feel there is promise for the global application of MI as a way to enhance a school's climate in addition to helping individual students with change, we would support any effort to incorporate MI-consistent conversations as a way to support student growth and ultimately improve student outcomes. Furthermore, some models have research support, whereas other models presented below are untested ideas that require more investigation.

Outside Help for Students

One common approach to integrating MI involves an outside group, often a university-based or nonprofit organization. Such a group is often called on to address problems certain students are experiencing, which may or may not relate directly to a school's mission. Outside groups have used MI to help students make positive changes with their schoolwork, such as to improve grades, as well as to help keep students from dropping out. Several programs also exist that are designed to help students with problems such as alcohol and other drug use, and chronic medical conditions such as diabetes and obesity. Of course, these areas of focus can impact academic performance in several ways; they just aren't the primary mission of schools. Partnerships between schools and community organizations can provide wonderful solutions for complex problems that schools may otherwise be poorly equipped to address, often due to lack of resources that place limitations on staffing numbers or training. Several examples of such programs exist.

Alternatives to In-School Suspension

Here's an example. A partnership between Northeastern Illinois University and the Chicago Public Schools takes high school students identified as most at risk, from several predominantly Latino or African American schools, and offers two creative alternatives to traditional punishment: (1) a 1-day program designed as a replacement for 1 day of in-school suspension (ISS); and (2) a 3-day program for students identified as most at risk (on the "hot list"). Both programs are grounded in MI and blended with (adventure-based) experiential education, to help support students to consider behavior change and to reengage in school.

Each day begins with playful cooperative activities and a shared agreement for the day (e.g., promoting respect and safety); followed by trust and problem-solving challenges, group discussions, and individual MI sessions provided by trained staff and graduate students; and concludes with a talking circle. The high school students typically find this experience valuable and school personnel often report a change even for the 1-day ISS experience. Evaluation data have suggested that the students in the alternative-to-ISS program are less likely to drop out by the next semester than students who only receive traditional ISS. And students on the "hot list" involved in the 3-day program show overall increases in grade point average, as well as comparatively better attendance than the schoolwide average (*www.centerforcollegeaccessandsuccess.org*).

Academic Performance

Here's an example of using MI in a single session with students. In a program designed to help middle school students (typically ages 12–14) believe in themselves and improve their schoolwork, researchers from the University of South Carolina (Strait et al., 2012) provided a single session of MI for over 100 students, most of them from ethnic minority groups. With the help of supportive graduate students trained in MI, students considered how much they believed in their abilities and how they assessed their positive academic behavior. The session also involved providing students with feedback about their goals and help in developing a change plan. Overall, even though the program involved only a single 50-minute session, students showed improvements in class participation and math grades.

Substance Use

A program called Guided Self-Change (GSC; Wagner, Hospital, Graziano, Morris, & Gil, 2014) involves a partnership between researchers at Florida International University and 16 Miami-area high schools to help primarily Hispanic and African American youth reduce alcohol and other drug use, as well as violent behavior. Master's-level counselors provide five individual treatment sessions for students within their schools. The program is grounded in a guiding style designed to help students set their own goals with counselor support, and to consider their level of importance and confidence in making changes. The program also combines an MI-based communication style with other therapeutic strategies to assist students in maintaining these changes.

Project CHOICE (D'Amico et al., 2012) is a voluntary after-school program for young teens interested in learning about and reducing their alcohol and other drug use (*http://groupmiforteens.org/programs/ choice*). This is a collaborative effort between the RAND Corporation and 16 middle schools in California. Using a flexible, five-session group-based approach to deliver MI, group leaders engage youth in discussions about substance use, role-play situations to help teens learn how to respond to peer pressure, and plan for so-called high-risk situations.

Childhood Obesity

Project Steps to Active Kids (STAK: Glazebrook et al., 2011) is an example of a school-based program to address the problem of childhood obesity by helping children become more physically active. This program is a partnership between the University of Nottingham in England and area primary schools involving students between 9 and 11 years old. There are multiple steps in the program, such as an activity diary, a dance DVD, and group classes in various exercise games. The students identified at greatest risk take part in an MI session(s) led by a researcher.

Another program targeting childhood obesity is called NEW MOVES (Flattum, Friend, Story, & Neumark-Sztainer, 2011). Researchers from the University of Minnesota partnered with several urban high schools to design a program specifically for teenage girls. Physical activity classes were combined with individual counseling sessions using MI and group lunch get-togethers.

These are just a sample of school-based programs involving out-side groups delivering creative MI-based interventions to help students grow in a number of areas. Notable components of these programs include:

- Brief interventions, often in a single session.
- A demonstration of the flexible nature of MI, used in individual and group environments.
- Combination of MI with other strategies.
- A broad age range, from 9 to 18.
- Support for student autonomy; students often have choices about whether to participate, as well as what areas they would like to change.
- Approaches consistent with the MI spirit.
- Guidance toward specific goals.

Growing MI from Within

Efforts to adopt an MI-based approach to help students can also arise and grow within the school itself, born from the creative energy of teachers and other staff. All it requires for such an effort to take hold is an individual teacher seeking to engage with and guide a student(s) facing a dilemma. Such efforts can involve carefully designed programs implemented by the school administration, or it can occur as most conversations do in schools all over the world, during quiet moments before or after school, amid the hectic energy of recess, or during class itself.

Individual Students

Individualized efforts are rarely published; however, Atkinson and Woods (2003) wrote a case example of an educational psychologist using MI to help a high school student experiencing a number of academic and behavioral challenges. The student received five sessions of MI, which helped her make specific changes in her academic behavior, but also led to improvements in her overall future outlook.

Self-Contained Programs

Many schools have self-contained programs to meet the needs of certain members of the student population, those often identified as having "special needs." In many instances these programs also function as free-standing schools. The students often experience significant challenges, both at school and in their communities, and such alternative programs tend to utilize a therapeutic model(s) to address emotional and behavioral difficulties along with the everyday task of learning. While we are familiar with some "second-chance" schools integrating MI, we are not familiar with any alternative schools that use MI as a core model to approach student conversations. We believe applying MI as a programwide model holds promise.

The program could incorporate MI training for all involved staff, teachers, counselors, secretaries, security officers, in fact, anyone with a role in the lives of the students they serve. Such training would focus both on applied skills and on ways of developing a strengths-based culture within the program. Students in alternative programs have often clashed with adults using punitive measures, either within their schools or even in the juvenile justice system, with little effect in helping students explore a more hopeful future. MI can be one of several strategies with an aim toward guiding students in new directions, building off strengths unearthed through skillful conversation.

Peer-Involved Programs

Peers can bring a unique perspective when counseling fellow students, but can they learn and integrate MI into this activity? Plasmawr School in Cardiff, Wales, used this approach to train older students to help younger ones adapt to their new school environment, with a focus on emotional intelligence, problem solving, and improving well-being (Channon, Marsh, Jenkins, & Robling, 2013). Topics commonly included relationships with classmates, exploring how to achieve their goals, staying out of trouble with teachers, or resolving ambivalence as they move toward independence.

A teacher commented, "We soon realized that by giving our children responsibility, leadership skills, that we were gaining so much from that . . . and the [mentors] were actually gaining so many skills it even impacted on behavior in classrooms, it impacted on the respect between adults and child, and between pupil and pupil" (in Channon et al., 2013, p. 74).

For the peer mentors it was generally a positive experience, boosting their confidence, helping them feel more mature, enhancing their communication skills, and making them more reflective including and broadening their thinking even about their careers. One student noted, "Yeah, you get a lot of respect from the teachers as well for being [a mentor] because it helps you communicate with everyone generally, they appreciate what you say as well." And another said, "It gives you more confidence and . . . you feel like you have done something to help the school and others in it. You feel more like a part of the school" (in Channon et al., 2013, p. 75).

The authors of the study believe that this peer support program made a significant contribution to the maintenance of the positive supportive school ethos that could be a model for other schools, suggesting that when there is synergy between the central tenets of MI and the ethos of the school, it enables schools to dovetail a mentoring effort with other aspects of the organization.

Whole-School MI Integration

Here we envision the use of MI throughout a school as part of an overall approach to the education of its students in which good relationships form the foundation for all else. No examples exist to our knowledge; however, we would expect a school that adopted MI as a primary communication approach would create a climate that was supportive of differences, nurturing for those who were struggling, and encouraging for those primed for academic success. In essence, it would be a place that incorporates all of the examples we've shared in this book. The use of MI can facilitate change in the context of learning, classroom behavior, peer interactions to reduce bullying and increase compassion between students, and conversations that address the future from whether to remain in school or whether to pursue school or a career after graduation. We would envision such a school as a community free of judgment and full of curiosity about learning and the potential of others. This is congruent with the path that many schools are on, some of which are incorporating restorative discipline practices and finding ways to incorporate autonomy support with guided learning experiences while maintaining a structure of rigor and high expectations.

Professional Development and Support

Assuming you feel there is potential for the use of MI in your school, you may be wondering, How do we get started? How can teacher(s), eager for a new approach or possibly for refining an old one, learn and practice MI? How could an administrator, intrigued at the possibility of more widespread MI integration to help support student change, secure training for his or her staff?

There are multiple tasks necessary to get started in supporting others to gain MI proficiency aimed at helping enhance student motivation to learn. By now you know the drawbacks of trying to demand interest. Instead, hopefully you'll be able to tap into the intrinsic motivation of those who see MI as a practical approach to help them deal with students more effectively. Generating buy-in and enthusiasm will help increase their willingness to learn, since their own change process must be up to them. So what will work to take on this task of helping others decide to want to learn MI? A solid leadership backing for this kind of effort is probably the first and most important factor. MI skills will help you do this.

Taking into account the politics, attitudes, and personalities involved is important. New programs and initiatives come and go, often take great effort to get underway, then sometimes are dropped or forgotten. Will MI be considered something like the "new kid on the block"? Will teachers and other staff feel they are being pushed to learn it against their will? Clearly, they need to see MI as useful and experience it as effective for them to invest in learning it.

> *Will teachers and other staff feel they are being coerced to learn MI?*

The framework of the four processes is useful for this effort. By taking time to involve your colleagues in engaging, focusing, evoking, and planning, you can increase the odds of a successful integration of MI into your school. Let's think through how to do this.

• *Engaging.* How can you create a collaborative, mutually respectful working relationship with those you wish to train in MI? How can it be possible to help others feel safe enough to be willing to divulge challenges they face with students? Will they have a say in deciding how, when, and where? Will there be options or will it come across as a mandate? How will it help them feel affirmed for their existing professional skills and experiences, particularly the strength-based, MI-adherent practices they already use?

• *Focusing.* What schoolwide outcome goals might it be possible to focus on to generate interest, support, and ownership? Do your colleagues want to achieve something that MI will help them do? Is there a shared sense of direction? Do they think it will make them more effective professionally? Does it make sense to explore how integrating MI could strengthen existing goals or outcomes?

• *Evoking.* How might you evoke teachers' opinions, feelings, or thoughts to resolve any ambivalence they have about learning MI? Will everyone feel autonomous and safe without feeling judged or evaluated to facilitate wanting to move ahead? How will sharing be encouraged about why it makes sense to learn MI? How committed are they to do what it will take?

 • *Planning.* How would it be possible to make the planning process participatory and inclusive, allowing everyone a voice and those interested in helping take leadership in organizing the process for learning MI? Since it is easy to fall back on being controlling by deciding what is best without input, what process will be in place to avoid this problem? Will there be mechanisms for feedback, for example, outcome data to determine efficacy and possibly create enthusiasm?

 The time that is taken to increase collaborative relationships and a sense of community, to provide choices, and to affirm and respect opinions and professional expertise is crucial. So, the process is important, regardless of the sequence and steps decided.

Tips for Administrators

MI can become a stand-alone schoolwide initiative or it can be used to improve other efforts, particularly strength-based ones that are congruent with the spirit of MI (discussed in Chapter 3). If the training process is mandatory, be mindful of the process and care that will be required to help get a core number of teachers and staff on board, so that they see it as inherently relevant to them. An appreciative inquiry (Cooperrider & Whitney, 2001) or other asset-based strategic planning process may be helpful, which could involve surveys, interviews, or focus groups. Processes that involve building on successes and incorporating an evidence-based model for behavior change as MI could do much to improve outcomes.

> *MI can become a stand-alone schoolwide initiative or it can be used to improve other efforts.*

Introducing MI

Initiatives in schools come and go, and it is easy to become cynical regarding new ones. The goal of integrating MI into professional practice will require generating interest, most likely through informal conversations. If there is a chance to make an introductory presentation, the four MI processes can be a blueprint. Within this presentation, it will be important to engage your listeners, help them focus on the reasons behind MI and benefits that MI could bring them, evoke their opinions and ideas, and welcome their involvement in planning the learning process. You may find the two group activities (the closed fist activity and the trials activity) described in Chapter 17 as a way to introduce and generate interest in MI.

Structuring the Learning

There are multiple options to consider regarding how to structure the opportunities for learning MI. Research suggests that mastering MI is not something that can happen with a single workshop, but requires that the learning continue over time, often involving coaching and feedback (Miller & Rollnick, 2013). Since people are different, there is not a one-size-fits-all approach. Workshops focusing on practicing can be an efficient way to introduce concepts and begin skill building. One study found that six individual coaching sessions that lasted for 30 minutes each (conducted by phone) was able to have trainees reach proficiency (Miller, Yahne, Moyers, Martinez, & Pirritano, 2004). It is for that reason that Miller and Rollnick (2013) suggest it may be sensible to develop on-site expertise in MI or at least—as described below—provide the time and support for an ongoing learning community.

Regardless of the actual sequence of learning MI, there are three experiential teaching tools that are important, providing opportunities to (1) listen to MI sessions; (2) practice MI; and (3) get feedback about MI. Becoming competent with MI has been compared to mastering a foreign language, which requires more than just learning the grammatical rules, but also considerable time hearing the new language and discovering its nuances. So, listening to or watching recorded MI sessions with experienced practitioners can be valuable. Reading and analyzing scenarios like you've experienced in this book or transcripts of sessions can be helpful. Taking time to practice using real-plays (practicing with other trainees using issues they feel true ambivalence about), role plays, or other activities to get better requires effort and participation. Coaching and guidance is helpful in making progress. An essential part of that is feedback that is affirming and allows for incremental acquisition of

MI skills. Building feedback into the structured skill-building opportunities will help speed the learning process, including, if possible, coded ratings from sessions (described below).

Yet, as described in Chapter 6, having learners practice MI with students and seeing the response to what they do can be the most valuable process.

As the plans are made to structure the learning opportunities, there are of course shortcomings that may result from trying to create a one-size-fits-all approach. Providing options to accommodate different needs or preferences is usually wise, particularly if MI use is being mandated. If you are in a position of authority, it may be important to express your expectation while explaining the reasons (because of the outcomes sought) and reassuring teachers and other school personnel that there will be choices provided for how to learn it, acknowledging that it is up to them.

Facilitating Self-Directed Learning

As one of the leading "take work home" professions, educators are busy, yet, as you know, they will take time to work on gaining practical skills to make their job more effective, easier, or more satisfying. This book is for educators, administrators, and anyone working in schools with children, adolescents, and young adults.

Having a resource shelf in the library, the staff lounge, or an accessible part of the school office with handouts, DVDs, and books will allow staff to check out resources if they want to. Providing opportunities for trainees to use feedback tools including listening and self-coding and having taped session coded (by experts preferably) are ways to help them increase their MI competency more rapidly. Linking them to professional learning communities on one of the web-based platforms can help them share challenges and learn from other MI practitioners.

MI Professional Development Learning Communities

Helping to organize professional development learning communities or study group(s) to learn MI is a way to help develop proficiency. The gatherings could begin as weekly or semimonthly meetings before or after school and go on for a predetermined period. It may be beneficial to attendees to be able to receive continuing professional development units, if that is possible. The following are some ideas for organizing peer support groups in schools:

1. Hour-long skill-strengthening sessions focused solely on MI practice.
2. Discussion of specific readings that members have done between meetings (see books and articles at *www.motivationalinterviewing.org*).
3. Using recordings, no longer than 20 minutes in length, of role plays involving group members re-creating conversations about school-related topics. The group can listen to the recordings and offer feedback to group members.
4. Listening to other recordings of MI sessions available online (on YouTube) or from training DVDs. Group members could code these recordings by counting the number of questions and reflections, taking note of the student's change talk, noting what preceded it, and so on.

Organizing Workshops, Seminars, or Institutes

One of the most efficient and common ways to initiate learning MI is to organize workshops, a series of seminars, or institutes. Clearly, workshops on professional development days can be opportune to introduce relevant concepts and practices of MI. Having workshops may mean bringing in experienced trainers. The Motivational Interviewing Network of Trainers (MINT) has over 1,200 active members worldwide with a wide distribution, making it possible to find someone geographically close. On the MINT website (*www.motivationalinterviewing.org*), in addition to the listing of trainers with experience in schools or social settings, there are descriptions of types of workshops and what to expect. It is also a place to find a listing of workshops from experienced trainers as well as how to become a trainer of trainers.

As with any new skill, unless what is being learned is reinforced, retaining it can diminish over time. Studies show that if an individual participates in a single workshop and does not review and have opportunities for reinforcement, in 2 months most of the understanding and skills will be lost. Of course, that can have lots to do with the interest of the person to review and practice. If you are the person in the role of leader to advocate and support the learning process, organizing various options to do this is ideal. Making books available to staff, and sending them links to websites and demonstrations, may be helpful, as is providing them with coaching.

Coaching Sessions

Coaching sessions provide a valuable way to review, reinforce, practice, and get immediate feedback. These involve either individual sessions or small groups that gather with the presence of an experienced MI practitioner. Coaching sessions sometimes focus on the everyday challenges of using MI in a particular situation or with particular students. Role-playing conversations provides practice and feedback on interactions. The experienced practitioner provides guidance for positive feedback from group members and, if appropriate, bite-size suggestions, all in an MI-adherent way. In addition to role-playing conversations that seemed difficult, coaching sessions can focus on a particular aspect of MI. Early sessions can focus on one of the core skills (OARS), and later sessions can address more complex strategies and approaches for understanding and dealing with discord, sustain talk, strengthening change talk, or recognizing and addressing commitment language.

Coding Feedback

Feedback is important and so, if possible, offering the most interested individuals the opportunity to have an MI session(s) coded for feedback would be very valuable. There are several tools and ways to do this which usually involve asking each person to submit a recording of up to 20 minutes of a session (real or role play) to an experienced coder or arranging to have learners do a phone session where they are recorded with an actor on the phone, for coding. An experienced MI trainer can usually arrange this. (See *www.motivationalinterviewing. org* for an international list of MI trainers.)

Consent from interviewees for recordings is necessary, which is easiest if the person is 18 or older (not requiring parental consent), which is why using a young adult actor (on the phone or in person) is sometimes helpful—even if it is less authentic than a recording of an actual conversation with a student. In the consent form, it should be made clear why and how the recording will be used (for improving the teacher's ability to communicate in a supportive way or fidelity), as well as who will listen to it and when it will be discarded. Schools may choose to create a form for this process, or add this language to the general consent forms required when parents enroll their children.

Recognizing Effort and Accomplishments

As we know, motivation for learning MI can be augmented by the conversations that take place. Affirming and acknowledging your colleagues' hard work, commitment, or skill progress can increase their feelings of competence and motivation to continue to learn MI. Indirect ways of doing this are by arranging or supporting opportunities for them to present about their experience using MI at meetings with colleagues, guests, or at conferences.

One of the challenges of any initiative like introducing MI is maintaining enthusiasm. Analyzing and sharing results or outcomes attributed (or partially attributed) to the use of MI with students can be particularly useful in promoting the value of learning it. With the growing push for data-driven change, carrying out evaluation or research on specific areas of focus (e.g., comparative data on attendance, retention, academic performance, improved grades or grade point average, incidences of tardiness or disruptive behavior) can make it clear that the effort is worth it. Even sharing stories or more formal qualitative feedback from educators using MI can be valuable. Organizing an action research project is an option to involve colleagues in this process.

Remember that everyone has a need to feel competent, and opportunities that reinforce competence enhance intrinsic motivation. So too do opportunities to create a sense of community while at the same time honoring autonomy. The process of helping others gain MI skills can become a model for what MI can look like with students, since it involves learning and change. By understanding that focusing on the process is as important as reaching the outcome, educators will be reminded how learning happens best, and the process of school change may unfold.

> *Helping others gain MI skills models MI with students, since it involves learning and change.*

References

Allensworth, E. M., & Easton, J. Q. (2005, June). The On-Track Indicator as a predictor of graduation. Retrieved August 6, 2015, from Consortium on Chicago School Research at the University of Chicago website: *www.scoe. net/calsoap/pages/Counselor%20Resource/OnTrackIndicator.pdf.*

Alliance for Excellent Education. (2011, November). Issue brief: The high cost for high school dropouts: What the nation pays for inadequate high schools. Retrieved August 6, 2015, from *http://all4ed.org/wpcontent/ uploads/2013/06/HighCost.pdf.*

Arnez, N. L. (1978). Implementation of desegregation as a discriminatory process. *Journal of Negro Education, 47,* 28–45.

Atkinson, C., & Woods, K. (2003). Motivational interviewing strategies for disaffected secondary school students: A case example. *Educational Psychology in Practice, 19,* 49–64.

Attinasi, L. C. (1989). Getting in: Mexican Americans' perceptions of university attendance and the implications for freshman year persistence. *Journal of Higher Education, 60,* 247–277.

Baker, J. P., & Crist, J. L. (1971). Teacher expectancies: A review of the literature. In J. D. Elashoff & R. E. Snow (Eds.), *Pygmalion reconsidered; A case study in statistical inference: Reconsideration of the Rosenthal–Jacobson data on teacher expectancy* (pp. 48–64). Worthington, OH: Charles A. Jones.

Barber, J. G., & Crisp, B. R. (1995). Social support and prevention of relapse following treatment for alcohol use. *Research and Social Work Practice, 5,* 283–296.

Barnett, E., Moyers, T. B., Sussman, S., Smith, C., Rohrbach, L. A., Sun, P., et al. (2014). From counselor skill to decreased marijuana use: Does change talk matter? *Journal of Substance Abuse Treatment, 46,* 498–505.

205

Bearden, L. J., Spencer, W. A., & Moracco, J. C. (1989). A study of high school dropouts. *School Counselor, 37,* 113–120.

Blaakman, S. W., Cohen, A., Fagnano, M., & Halterman, J. S. (2014). Asthma medication adherence among urban teens: A qualitative analysis of barriers, facilitators and experiences with school-based care. *Journal of Asthma, 51,* 522–529.

Bonde, A. H., Bentsen, P., & Hindhede, A. L. (2014). School nurses' experiences with motivational interviewing for preventing childhood obesity. *Journal of School Nursing, 30,* 448–455.

Braxton, J. M. (1995). Expectations for college and student persistence. *Research in Higher Education, 36,* 595–612.

Brendtro, L. K., Mitchell, M. L., & McCall, H. J. (2009). *Deep brain learning: Pathways to potential with challenging youth.* Circle of Courage, Battle Creek, MI: Starr Commonwealth.

Bridgeland, J. M., DiIulio Jr., J. J., & Morison, K. B. (2006, March). The silent epidemic: Perspectives of high school dropouts. Retrieved January 18, 2014, from Civic Enterprises in Association with Peter D. Hart Research Associates for the Bill and Melinda Gates Foundation at *http://files.eric.ed.gov/fulltext/ED513444.pdf.*

Buchmann, C., & DiPrete, T. A. (2006). The growing female advantage in college completion: The role of family background and academic achievement. *American Sociological Review, 71,* 515–541.

Carnevale, A. P., & Strohl, J. (2013, July). Separate and unequal: How higher education reinforces the intergenerational reproduction of white racial privilege. Retrieved December 7, 2014, from Georgetown University, Public Policy Institute, Center on Education and the Workforce website at *https://cew.georgetown.edu/separateandunequal.*

Center for Public Education. (2010, April 5). Keeping kids in school: What research says about preventing dropouts. Retrieved August 29, 2014, from *www.centerforpubliceducation.org/Main-Menu/Staffingstudents/Keeping-kids-in-school-At-a-glance/Keeping-kids-in-school-Preventing-dropouts.html.*

Channon, S., Marsh, K., Jenkins, A., & Robling, M. (2013). Using motivational interviewing as the basis for a peer support programme in high school. *Pastoral Care in Education, 31,* 66–78.

Chirkov, V. I., & Ryan, R. M. (2001). Parent and teacher autonomy-support in Russian and US adolescents: Common effects on well-being and academic motivation. *Journal of Cross-Cultural Psychology, 32,* 618–635.

Cook, C. R., Williams, K. R., Guerra, N. G., & Kim, T. E. (2010). Variability in the prevalence of bullying and victimization: A cross-national and methodological analysis. In S. R. Jimmerson, S. M. Swearer, & D. L. Espelage (Eds.), *Handbook of bullying in schools: An international perspective* (pp. 347–362). New York: Routledge.

Cooperrider, D. L., & Whitney, D. (2001). *Appreciative inquiry: A positive revolution in change.* San Francisco: Berrett-Koehler.

Copeland, W. E., Wolke, D., Angold, A., & Costello, E. J. (2013). Adult psychiatric outcomes of bullying and being bullied by peers in childhood and adolescence. *JAMA Psychiatry, 70,* 419–426.

Corbett, G. (2009, November). What the research says . . . about the "MI spirit" and the "competence worldview." *Motivational Interviewing Network of Trainers (MINT) Bulletin, 15,* 3–5. Retrieved August 1, 2015, from *www. motivationalinterviewing.org/sites/default/files/MINT15_1.pdf.*

Cornell, D. G., & Bandyopadhyay, S. (2010). The assessment of bullying. In S. R. Jimmerson, S. M. Swearer, & D. L. Espelage (Eds.), *Handbook of bullying in schools: An international perspective* (pp. 265–276). New York: Routledge.

Cozolino, L. (2013). *The social neuroscience of education: Optimizing attachment and learning in the classroom (The Norton Series on the Social Neuroscience of Education).* New York: Norton.

D'Amico, E. J., Tucker, J. S., Miles, J. N. V., Zhou, A. J., Shih, R. A., & Green, H. D. (2012). Preventing alcohol use with a voluntary after-school program for middle school students: Results from a cluster randomized controlled trial of CHOICE. *Prevention Science, 13,* 415–425.

Datiri, D. H. (2013, July 6). No Child Left Behind and dropout recovery: Making a diploma count. *Teachers College Record.* Retrieved August 7, 2015, from *www.tcrecord.org/Content.asp?ContentId=17175.*

Daugherty, M. D. (2003). *A randomized trial of motivational interviewing with college students for academic success.* Ph.D. dissertation, University of New Mexico, Albuquerque, NM.

deCharmes, R. (1968). *Personal causation.* New York: Academic Press.

deCharmes, R., Shea, D. J., Jackson, K. W., Plimpton, F., Koenigs, S., & Blasi, A. (1976). *Enhancing motivation: Change in the classroom.* New York: Irvington.

Dunn, C., Chambers, D., & Rabren, K. (2004). Variables affecting students' decisions to drop out of school. *Remedial and Special Education, 25,* 314–323.

Dweck, C. (2006). *Mindset: How you can fulfill your potential.* New York: Random House.

Dynarski, M., Clarke, L., Cobb, B., Finn, J., Rumberger, R., & Smink, J. (2008). *Dropout prevention: A practice guide* (NCEE 2008-4025). Washington, DC: National Center for Education Evaluation and Regional Assistance, Institute of Education Sciences, U.S. Department of Education. Retrieved from *http://ies.ed.gov/ncee/wwc.*

Enea, V., & Dafinoiu, I. (2009). Motivational/solution-focused intervention for reducing school truancy among adolescents. *Journal of Cognitive and Behavioral Psychotherapies, 9,* 186–198.

Farrington, C. A., Roderick, M., Allensworth, E., Nagaoka, J., Keyes, T. S., Johnson, D. W., et al. (2012). *Teaching adolescents to become learners: The role of noncognitive factors in shaping school performance: A critical literature review.* Chicago: University of Chicago Consortium on Chicago School Research.

Fekkes, M., Pijpers, F. I. M., Fredriks, A. M., Vogels, T., & Verloove-Vanhorick, S. (2006). Do bullied children get ill, or do ill children get bullied?: A prospective cohort study on the relationship between bullying and health-related symptoms. *Pediatrics, 117,* 1568–1574.

Finn, J. D. (1989). Withdrawing from school. *Review of Educational Research,* *59,* 117–142.

Flattum, C., Friend, S., Story, M., & Neumark-Sztainer, D. (2011). Evaluation of an individualized counseling approach as part of a multicomponent school-based program to prevent weight-related problems among adolescent girls. *Journal of the American Dietetic Association, 111,* 1218–1223.

Ford, M. E. (1987). Processes contributing to adolescent social competence. In M. E. Ford & D. H. Ford (Eds.), *Humans as self-constructing living systems: Putting the framework to work* (pp. 199–233). Hillsdale, NJ: Erlbaum.

Frank, L. S. (2013). *Journey toward the caring classroom: Using adventure to create community in the classroom and beyond, 2nd edition.* Bethany, OK: Wood N' Barnes.

Garrity, C., Jens, K., Porter, W., Sager, N., & Short-Camilli, C. (1994). *Bully-proofing your school.* Longmont, CO: Sopris West.

Glazebrook, C., Batty, M. J., Mullan, N., MacDonald, I., Nathan, D., Sayal, K., et al. (2011). Evaluating the effectiveness of a schools-based programme to promote exercise self-efficacy in children and young people with risk factors for obesity: Steps to active kids (STAK). *BMC Public Health, 11,* 830.

Gonzalez-DeHass, A. R., Willems, P. P., & Holbein, M. F. D. (2005). Examining the relationship between parental involvement and student motivation. *Educational Psychology Review, 17,* 99–123.

Gordon, T. (2003). *Teacher effectiveness training: The program proven to help teachers bring out the best in students of all ages.* New York: Three Rivers Press.

Gray, P. (2011). The decline of play and the rise of psychopathology in children and adolescents. *American Journal of Play, 3,* 443–463.

Hall, B., Stewart, D. G., Arger, C., Athenour, D. R., & Effinger, J. (2014). Modeling motivation three ways: Effects of MI metrics on treatment outcomes among adolescents. *Psychology of Addictive Behaviors, 28,* 307–312.

Hamilton, G., O'Connell, M., & Cross, D. (2004). Adolescent smoking cessation: Development of a school nurse intervention. *Journal of School Nursing, 20,* 169–174.

Herman, K. C., Frey, A. J., Shephard, S. A., & Reinke, W. M. (2013). *Motivational interviewing in schools: Strategies for engaging parents, teachers, and students.* New York: Springer.

Herrán, C. A., & Van Uythem, B. (2001, July). Why do youngsters drop out of school in Argentina and what can be done against it? Inter-American Development Bank. Retrieved August 7, 2015, from *www.mineducacion. gov.co/1621/articles-85774_archivo_pdf1.pdf.*

Hettema, J., Steele, J., & Miller, W. R. (2005). Motivational interviewing. *Annual Review of Clinical Psychology, 1,* 91–111.

Hinton, C., Fischer, K. W., & Glennon, C. (2012, March). The Students at the Center Series: Mind, brain, and education. Jobs for the Future. Retrieved August 7, 2015, from *www.studentsatthecenter.org/sites/scl.dl-dev.com/ files/Mind%20Brain%20Education.pdf.*

Jang, H., Reeve, J., & Deci, E. L. (2010). Engaging students in learning activities:

It is not autonomy support or structure but autonomy support and structure. *Journal of Educational Psychology, 102,* 588–600.

Jimerson, S. R., Swearer, S. M., & Espelage, D. L. (Eds.). (2010). *Handbook of bullying in schools: An international perspective.* New York: Routledge.

Kanfer, F. H. (1970). Self-monitoring: Methodological limitations and clinical applications. *Journal of Consulting and Clinical Psychology, 35,* 148–158.

Kelly, D. M. (1993). *Last chance high: How girls and boys drop in and out of alternative schools.* New Haven, CT: Yale University Press.

Kim, C., Losen, D., & Hewitt, D. (2010). *The school-to-prison pipeline: Structuring legal reform.* New York: New York University Press.

Kortering, L. J., Braziel, P. M., & Tompkins, J. R. (2002). The challenge of school completion among youths with behavioral disorders: Another side of the story. *Behavioral Disorders, 27,* 142–154.

Lamb, S., Markussen, E., Teese, R., Sandberg, N., & Polesel, J. (Eds.). (2010). *School dropout and completion: International comparative studies in theory and policy.* New York: Springer Science & Business Media.

Lee, T., Cornell, D., Gregory, A., & Fan, X. (2011). High suspension schools and dropout rates for black and white students. *Education and Treatment of Children, 34,* 167–192.

Leonhardt, D. (2014, May 27). Is college worth it?: Clearly new data say. *New York Times.* Retrieved November 27, 2014, from *www.nytimes. com/2014/05/27/upshot/is-college-worth-it-clearly-new-data-say.html?_ r=0&abt=0002&abg=0.*

Levin, H. M. (1986). *Educational reform for disadvantaged students.* Washington, DC: National Education Association.

Longabaugh, R., Wirtz, P. W., Zweben, A., & Stout, R. L. (1998). Network support for drinking: Alcoholics Anonymous and long-term matching effects. *Addiction, 93,* 1313–1333.

Losen, D. J. (2011, October 5). Discipline policies, successful schools, and racial justice. *National Educational Policy Center.* Retrieved August 7, 2015, from *http://nepc.colorado.edu/publication/discipline-policies.*

Losen, D. J., & Gillespie, J. (2012, August 7). Opportunities suspended: The disparate impact of disciplinary exclusion from school. *The Civil Rights Project/Proyecto Derechos Civiles.* Retrieved January 17, 2015, from *http://civilrightsproject.ucla.edu/resources/projects/center-for-civil-rights-remedies/school-to-prison-folder/federal-reports/upcoming-ccrr-research/losen-gillespie-opportunity-suspended-2012.pdf.*

Miller, W. R., C'de Baca, J., Matthews, D. B., & Wilbourne, P. L. (2001). Personal values card sort. Retrieved August 7, 2015, from *www.motivationalinterviewing.org/sites/default/files/valuescardsort_0.pdf.*

Miller, W. R., & Rollnick, S. (2013). *Motivational interviewing: Helping people change* (3rd ed.). New York: Guilford Press.

Miller, W. R., & Rose, G. S. (2015). Motivational interviewing and decisional balance: Contrasting responses to client ambivalence. *Behavioural and Cognitive Psychotherapy, 43,* 129–141.

Miller, W. R., Sovereign, R. G., & Krege, B. (1988). Motivational interviewing with problem drinkers: II. The drinker's check-up as a preventive intervention. *Behavioural Psychotherapy, 16,* 251–268.

Miller, W. R., Yahne, C. E., Moyers, T. B., Martinez, J., & Pirritano, M. (2004). A randomized trial of methods to help clinicians learn motivational interviewing. *Journal of Consulting and Clinical Psychology, 72,* 1050–1062.

Naar-King, S., & Suarez, M. (2011). *Motivational interviewing with adolescents and young adults.* New York: Guilford Press.

Nansel, T. R., Overpeck, M., Pilla, R. S., Ruan, W. J., Simons-Morton, B., & Schedit, P. (2001). Bullying behaviors among US youth: Prevalence and association with psychosocial adjustment. *Journal of the American Medical Association, 285,* 2094–2100.

National Center for Education Statistics. (2014). Fast facts: Back to school statistics. Retrieved October 23, 2014, from *http://nces.ed.gov/fastfacts/display.asp?id=372.*

Newmann, F. M. (1981). Reducing student alienation in high schools: Implications of theory. *Harvard Educational Review, 51,* 546–564.

Olweus, D. (1993). *Bullying at school: What we know and what we can do.* Cambridge, MA: Blackwell.

Olweus, D., & Limber, S. P. (2010). The Olweus Bullying Prevention Program: Implementation and evaluation over two decades. In S. R. Jimmerson, S. M. Swearer, & D. L. Espelage (Eds.), *Handbook of bullying in schools: An international perspective* (pp. 377–401). New York: Routledge.

Orfield, G. (Ed.). (2004). *Dropouts in America: Confronting the graduation rate crisis.* Cambridge, MA: Harvard Education Publishing Group.

Porter, W., Plog, A., Jens, K., Garrity, C., & Sager, N. (2010). Bully-proofing your elementary school: Creating a caring community. In S. R. Jimmerson, S. M. Swearer, & D. L. Espelage (Eds.), *Handbook of bullying in schools: An international perspective* (pp. 431–440). New York: Routledge.

Public Policy Institute, Center on Education and the Workforce. (2013). Recovery: Job growth and education requirements through 2020, Georgetown University, June 2013, executive summary. Retrieved from *https://cew.georgetown.edu/recovery2020.*

Reeve, J. (1995). *Motivating others: Nurturing inner motivational resources.* Needham Heights, MA: Allyn & Bacon.

Reid, K. C. (1981). Alienation and persistent school absenteeism. *Research in Education, 26,* 31–40.

Rigby, K. (2013). Bullying interventions. *Every Child Journal, 3*(5), 70–75.

Rigby, K., & Bauman, S. (2010). How school personnel tackle cases of bullying: A critical examination. In S. R. Jimmerson, S. M. Swearer, & D. L. Espelage (Eds.), *Handbook of bullying in schools: An international perspective* (pp. 455–467). New York: Routledge.

Robbins, L. B., Pfeiffer, K. A., Maier, K. S., LaDrig, S. M., & Berg-Smith, S. M. (2012). Treatment fidelity of motivational interviewing delivered by a school nurse to increase girls' physical activity. *Journal of School Nursing, 28,* 70–78.

Robbins, L. B., Pfeiffer, K. A., Wesolek, S. M., & Lo, Y. (2013). Process evaluation for a school-based physical activity intervention for 6th- and 7th-grade boys: Reach, dose, and fidelity. *Evaluation and Program Planning, 42*, 21–31.

Robinson, K. (2014, August 6). The educators (BBC Radio 4 program). Available at *www.bbc.co.uk/programmes/P0249h5b*.

Robinson, M. (2014, October). 11–18 play in secondary schools: The research behind play in schools. *Inspiring Scotland*. Retrieved August 7, 2015, from *www.ltl.org.uk/pdf/The-value-of-play-in-11-18-secondary-schools1429 523246.pdf*.

Rogers, C. (1980). *A way of being*. New York: Houghton Mifflin.

Rosengren, D. (2009). *Building motivational interviewing skills: A practitioner workbook*. New York: Guilford Press.

Rosenthal, R., & Jacobson, L. (1968). Pygmalion in the classroom. *Urban Review, 3*, 16–20.

Rouse, C. E. (2005, October). *The labor market consequences of inadequate education*. Paper presented at the 2005 Symposium "The Social Costs of Inadequate Education," The Campaign for Educational Equity at Teachers College. Retrieved August 7, 2015, from *www.literacycooperative.org/documents/TheLaborMarketConsequencesofanInadequateEd.pdf*.

Ryan, R. M., & Deci, E. L. (2000). Self-determination theory and the facilitation of intrinsic motivation, social development, and well-being. *American Psychologist, 55*, 68–78.

Safren, S. A., Otto, M. W., Worth, J. L., Salomon, E., Johnson, W., Mayer, K., et al. (2001). Two strategies to increase adherence to HIV antiretroviral medication: Life-steps and medication monitoring. *Behaviour Research and Therapy, 39*, 1151–1162.

Schomburg, H., & Teichler, U. (2006). *Higher education and graduate employment in Europe: Results from graduates surveys from twelve countries*. New York: Springer.

Siegal, D. (2013). *Brainstorm the power and the purpose of the teenage brain*. New York: Penguin.

Sinclair, M. F., Christenson, S. L., & Thurlow, M. L. (2005). Promoting school completion of urban secondary youth with emotional or behavioral disabilities. *Exceptional Children, 71*, 465–482.

Snape, L., & Atkinson, C. (2016). The evidence for student-focused motivational interviewing in educational settings: A review of the literature. *Advances in School Mental Health Promotion, 9*, 1–21.

Stage, F. K., & Hossler, D. (2000). Where is the student?: Linking student behaviors, college choice, and college persistence. In J. M. Braxton (Ed.), *Reworking the student departure puzzle* (pp. 170–194). Nashville, TN: Vanderbilt University Press.

Stetser, M., & Stillwell, R. (2014). *Public high school four-year on-time graduation rates and event dropout rates: School years 2010–11 and 2011–12*. First Look (NCES 2014-391). U.S. Department of Education. Washington, DC: National Center for Education Statistics. Retrieved August 9, 2015, from *http://nces.ed.gov/pubs2014/2014391.pdf*.

Strait, G. G., McQuillin, S., Terry, J., & Smith, B. H. (2014). School-based motivational interviewing with students, teachers, and parents: New developments and future direction. *Advances in School Mental Health Promotion, 7,* 205–207.

Strait, G. G., Smith, B. H., McQuillin, S., Terry, J., Swan, S., & Malone, P. S. (2012). A randomized trial of motivational interviewing to improve middle school students' academic performance. *Journal of Community Psychology, 40,* 1032–1039.

Sum, A., Khatiwada, I., & McLaughlin, J. (2009, October). The consequences of dropping out of high school: Joblessness and jailing for high school dropouts and the high cost for taxpayers. Retrieved August 9, 2015, from Northeastern University, Center for Labor Market Studies website: *www.northeastern.edu/clms/wpcontent/uploads/The_Consequences_of_Dropping_Out_of_High_School.pdf.*

Terry, J., Smith, B., Strait, G., & McQuillin, S. (2013). Motivational interviewing to improve middle school students' academic performance: A replication study. *Journal of Community Psychology, 42,* 902–909.

Terry, J., Strait, G., McQuillin, S., & Smith, B. (2014). Dosage effects of motivational interviewing on middle-school students' academic performance: Randomised evaluation of one versus two sessions. *Advances in School Mental Health Promotion, 7,* 62–74.

Test, D. W., Mazzotti, V. L., Mustian, A. L., Fowler, C. H., Kortering, L., & Kohler, P. (2009). Evidence-based secondary transition predictors for improving postschool outcomes for students with disabilities. *Career Development for Exceptional Individuals, 32*(3), 160–181.

Tidwell, R. (1988). Dropouts speak out: Qualitative data on early school departures. *Adolescence, 23,* 939–954.

Tinto, V., & Wallace, D. L. (1986). Retention: An admission concern. *College and University, 61,* 290–293.

Toshalis, E., & Nakkula, M. J. (2012). The Students at the Center Series: Motivation, engagement, and student voice. Jobs for the Future. Retrieved February 9, 2015, from *www.studentsatthecenter.org/sites/scl.dl-dev.com/files/Motivation%20Engagement%20Student%20Voice_0.pdf.*

Ttofi, M. M., & Farrington, D. P. (2011). Effectiveness of school-based programs to reduce bullying: A systematic and meta-analytic review. *Journal of Experimental Criminology, 7,* 27–56.

Tuck, E. (2012). *Urban youth and school pushout: Gateways, get-aways, and the GED.* New York: Routledge.

Twemlow, S. W., Fonagy, P., Sacco, F. C., Gies, M. L., Evans, R., & Ewbank, R. (2001). Creating a peaceful learning environment: A controlled study of an elementary school intervention to reduce violence. *American Journal of Psychiatry, 158,* 808–810.

Vallerand, R. J., & Bissonnette, R. (1992). Intrinsic, extrinsic, and amotivational styles as predictors of behavior: A prospective study. *Journal of Personality, 60,* 599–620.

Vallerand, R. J., Fortier, M. S., & Guay, F. (1997). Self-determination and persistence in a real-life setting: Toward a motivational model of high school dropout. *Journal of Personality and Social Psychology, 72,* 1161–1176.

Vansteenkiste, M., Mouratidis, A., & Lens, W. (2005). Detaching reasons from aims: Fair play and well-being in soccer as a function of pursuing performance-approach goals for autonomous or controlling reasons. *Journal of Sport and Exercise Psychology, 32,* 217–242.

Wagner, C. C., & Ingersoll, K. S. (2012). *Motivational interviewing in groups.* New York: Guilford Press.

Wagner, E. F., Hospital, M. M., Graziano, J. N., Morris, S. L., & Gil, A. G. (2014). A randomized controlled trial of guided self-change with minority adolescents. *Journal of Consulting and Clinical Psychology, 82,* 1128–1139.

Wehlage, G. G. (1983). *Effective programs for the marginal high school student: Fastback 197* (Report No. ISBN-0-87367-197-X). Bloomington, IN: Phi Delta Kappa Educational Foundation. (ERIC Document Reproduction Service No. ED235132)

Wehlage, G. G. (1989). *Reducing the risk: Schools as communities of support.* New York: Falmer Press.

Wehlage, G. G., & Rutter, R. A. (1986a). Dropping out: How much do schools contribute to the problem? *Teachers College Record, 87,* 374–392.

Wehlage, G. G., & Rutter, R. A. (1986b). *Evaluation of model programs for at risk students.* Paper presented at the annual meeting of the American Educational Research Association, San Francisco, CA.

What Kids Can Do, Inc. (2004, October). Students as allies in improving their schools: A report on work in progress. Retrieved August 9, 2015, from *www.whatkidscando.org/featurestories/2011/10_students_as_allies _2011/pdfs/saa_finalreport.pdf.*

Winsper, C., Lereya, T., Zanarini, M., & Wolke, D. (2012). Involvement in bullying and suicide-related behavior at 11 years: A prospective birth cohort study. *Journal of the American Academy of Child and Adolescent Psychiatry, 51,* 271–282.

Index

Note. *f* following a page number indicates a figure.

Absenteeism, 148, 150–151. *See also*
Dropout prevention; Truancy
Academic behavior. *See also* At-risk
students; Behavior; Learning
communication with parents or other
family members and, 121–124
dropout prevention and, 149–150,
151–152
how MI might help with, 88–100,
107–110
integrating MI in schools and, 193–
194
overview, 87–88
transitioning out of school and,
159–160
Acceptance
of ambivalence, 54–55
behavioral problems and, 86
conversations and, 14–15
learning MI and, 172–173, 174
personal growth and, 110, 111
planning and, 61
spirit of MI and, 24, 25
Achievements, 36, 121–124
Action plans, 54. *See also* Planning
Active learning, 8. *See also* Learning
Active listening, 39. *See also* Listening;
Reflection
Administration, 197–199
Advice giving
autonomy, relatedness, and competence
needs and, 64–65, 66–67

elicit–provide–elicit framework and,
63–66
overview, 60, 62–63, 67
Affirmations. *See also* Core conversational
skills; OARS skills
behavioral problems and, 80, 83, 84, 85
bullying and, 136
change talk and, 49–51, 53
classwide discussions and, 97, 98
communication with parents or other
family members and, 119, 123,
126–128
culturally diverse students and, 155
dropout prevention and, 152
learning and, 89, 90, 91–92, 95, 96–97
learning MI and, 172–173, 178–180,
181, 204
motivational interviewing in schools
and, 8
overview, 17, 33, 36–37, 42
personal growth and, 105, 107, 108,
109, 110, 113
planning and, 57, 61
transitioning out of school and,
164–165
Aggression, 132. *See also* Behavior;
Bullying; Fighting behaviors
Ambivalence. *See also* Double-sided
reflection
acceptance of, 54–55
behavioral problems and, 81
classwide discussions and, 97

Ambivalence (*continued*)
  evocation and, 46, 51, 53
  learning and, 88–89, 90
  overview, 5–6, 13
  personal growth and, 103–104, 105
  planning and, 54–55, 61
  transitioning out of school and,
    158–159
Anger problems, 79–86, 124–128
Applications of MI, 129. *See also* At-risk
    students; Behavior; Bullying;
    Dropout prevention; Families;
    Learning; Learning MI; Personal
    development; Practical applications
    of MI; Reengagement with school;
    Transition to life after school
Arguments, 45–46, 53
Art therapy, 145
Asking permission. *See* Permission
At-risk students. *See also* Academic
    behavior; Applications of MI;
    Cultural factors; Dropout prevention;
    Environment; Learning
  how MI might help with, 142–145
  integrating MI in schools and, 193,
    195–196
  nonpunitive approaches and, 143–
    145
  overview, 139–140, 145, 149
  principles of good practice and,
    140–142
  transitioning out of school and, 161
Attendance. *See* Absenteeism; Lateness;
    Truancy
Attending to student behavior, 3–4. *See
    also* Behavior
Autonomy
  acceptance and, 25
  at-risk students and, 141, 143, 144–
    145
  behavioral problems and, 84
  communication with parents or other
    family members and, 123
  culturally diverse students and, 155
  dropout prevention and, 149, 151
  giving information and advice and,
    64–65, 66–67
  learning and, 92–93, 96
  learning MI and, 186–188
  motivational interviewing in schools
    and, 8–9
  personal growth and, 107, 109, 114
  planning and, 55

B
Backtracking, 55–56
Barriers to success, 59–60, 61, 150–151

Behavior. *See also* Academic behavior;
    Applications of MI; Attending
    to student behavior; Practical
    applications of MI
  dropout prevention and, 148
  how MI might help with, 74–86,
    110–115
  integrating MI in schools and, 197
  overview, 73–74, 86
  personal growth and, 110–115
Behavioral support, 141
Belongingness, 149, 152
Blame
  behavioral problems and, 73–74, 80,
    83
  communication with parents or other
    family members and, 118
  personal growth and, 111
Boredom, 151
Bully Proofing Your School (BPYS), 134
Bullying. *See also* Applications of MI; Peer
    relationships
  how MI might help with, 135–138
  integrating MI in schools and, 197
  nonpunitive approaches and, 143
  overview, 131–134, 138
  responses to, 134–135

C
Change. *See also* Change talk; Motivation
  how MI might help with, 97–100
  learning and, 88, 101
  making a change plan, 57–60
  overview, 11–13, 53
  planning and, 54–57
Change plan, 57–60. *See also* Planning
Change talk. *See also* Conversations;
    Evocation; Motivation; Motivational
    interviewing (MI) in general; Sustain
    talk
  at-risk students and, 142
  behavioral problems and, 81, 84–85
  bullying and, 137
  classwide discussions and, 100
  communication with parents or other
    family members and, 120, 123–124
  dropout prevention and, 152–153, 154
  evocation and, 46–50, 53
  evoking and, 30–31, 44–45
  learning and, 90–91, 95, 96
  learning MI and, 184–186
  noticing, 42–43
  overview, 6–7, 17
  personal growth and, 105, 106, 108,
    109, 112–113, 115
  planning and, 55, 61
  reflection and, 39, 51

spirit of MI and, 25–26
transitioning out of school and,
    164–165
Change window, 79
Childhood obesity, 194–195
Choice
    advice giving and, 66–67
    autonomy, relatedness, and competence
        needs and, 64–65
    behavioral problems and, 78
    dropout prevention and, 151
    learning and, 89, 94, 96
    making a change plan and, 57–58
    personal growth and, 103, 109
    transitioning out of school and, 158–159
Classroom environment, 144–145. See also
    Environment
Classwide discussions, 92–100, 101
Closed questions, 34–35
Coaching, 22–23, 200, 203
Cognitive-behavioral approaches, 143–144
Collaboration, 25. See also Partnership
Collaborative conversation style, 12. See
    also Conversations
College. See also Transition to life after
    school
    dropout prevention and, 151
    how MI might help with the transition
        to, 160–165
    overview, 159–160
"Coming alongside" concept, 13–14
Commitment language. See also Change
    talk
    dropout prevention and, 154
    making a change plan and, 58
    overview, 47
    planning and, 61
Communication styles. See also Directing
    style of communication; Following
    style of communication; Guiding style
    of communication
    at-risk students and, 143
    behavioral problems and, 75
    overview, 20–21
Community, sense of, 149
Compassion, 24, 172–173, 174, 197
Competence
    dropout prevention and, 149
    giving information and advice and,
        64–65, 66–67
    making a change plan and, 57
    planning and, 55
Complex reflection, 40, 42. See also
    Reflection
Confidence, 88–92, 110
Confidence of change, 48–49. See also
    Change

Conflict resolution
    communication with parents or other
        family members and, 124–128
    how MI might help with, 82–86
    nonpunitive approaches and, 143
Consequences, 79
Conversational patterns, 27. See
    also Conversations; Engaging
    conversational pattern; Evoking
    conversational pattern; Focusing
    conversational pattern; Planning
    conversational pattern
Conversations. See also Change talk;
    Conversational patterns; Core
    conversational skills
    acceptance and curiosity and, 14–15
    combining core skills in, 41, 42
    empathy and, 33–34
    motivational interviewing in schools
        and, 8–9
    overview, 3, 6–7, 12–13
    pace of, 34
    personal growth and, 107
    restorative justice and, 143
Core conversational skills. See also
    Affirmations; Conversations; OARS
    skills; Open questions; Reflection;
    Summarization
    combining in conversations, 41, 42
    communication with parents or other
        family members and, 121–124
    empathy and, 33–34
    learning MI and, 172–173
    motivational interviewing and, 41–43
    overview, 17, 33, 42
    planning and, 57, 61
Counterarguments, 46
Creating a Peaceful School Learning
    Environment (CAPSLE), 134
Criminal behavior, 110–115. See also
    Behavior
Criticism, 118
Cultural factors. See also At-risk students
    bullying and, 132–133
    dropout prevention and, 148
    how MI might help with, 154–155
    motivational interviewing in schools
        and, 8
Curiosity. See also Evocation
    behavioral problems and, 75
    conversations and, 14–15
    giving information and advice and, 67
    learning MI and, 180–182
    personal growth and, 104–105, 111,
        112
    reflection and, 39
    spirit of MI and, 25–26

D

Decisional balance, 162–163
Defensiveness, 111
Delinquency, 110–115, 147, 148
Directing style of communication. *See also*
    Communication styles
    behavioral problems and, 75, 76–77, 78
    classwide discussions and, 97–98
    overview, 21, 22
    personal growth and, 114, 115
Discipline, 6, 193
Disempowerment, 55–56
Disruptive behavior, 79–82, 148
Double-sided reflection. *See also*
    Ambivalence; Reflection
    behavioral problems and, 81
    classwide discussions and, 98
    evocation and, 51
    learning and, 90
    overview, 40, 42
    personal growth and, 105, 108
Dropout prevention. *See also*
    Applications of MI; At-risk students;
    Reengagement with school
    culturally diverse students and, 154–
    155
    how MI might help with, 150–156
    overview, 146–148, 156–157
    research literature on, 148–150

E

Early intervention, 141
Efforts, 36
Elicit–provide–elicit framework. *See also*
    Advice giving; Information, providing
    autonomy, relatedness, and competence
    needs and, 64–65
    communication with parents or other
    family members and, 118–119, 120
    learning and, 88–89, 90, 92–97
    overview, 63–64
    personal growth and, 107
    scenarios utilizing, 65–66
Emotional intelligence, 196
Empathy
    bullying and, 138
    learning MI and, 172–174
    reflection and, 38, 39
    role of, 33–34
Employment following school, 159–160.
    See also Transition to life after school
Empowerment, 55–56
Encouragement, 88–89, 91–92
Engagement
    behavioral problems and, 75, 84, 86
    bullying and, 135–137
    classwide discussions and, 97, 99

    communication with parents or other
        family members and, 118
    dropout prevention and, 151
    empathy and, 34
    evocation and, 45–46, 53
    integrating MI in schools and, 198
    learning and, 89, 96
    learning MI and, 177–178
    personal growth and, 103, 104–105,
        110, 112
Engaging conversational pattern. *See also*
    Conversational patterns
    advice giving and, 66
    behavioral problems and, 79
    overview, 27–29, 28*f*
Environment. *See also* At-risk students
    behavioral problems and, 73
    dropout prevention and, 152
    overview, 140, 144–145
Evocation. *See also* Change talk; Evoking
    conversational pattern; Guiding style
    of communication
    at-risk students and, 142
    behavioral problems and, 81
    bullying and, 137, 137–138
    guidelines for, 45–53
    integrating MI in schools and, 198–199
    learning and, 89, 91
    learning MI and, 171–172, 173–174,
        177–178
    making a change plan and, 58
    overview, 8, 15–18, 44–45
    personal growth and, 106, 107, 114
    planning and, 54–57
    spirit of MI and, 24, 25–26
Evoking conversational pattern, 27, 30–31,
    30*f*. *See also* Conversational patterns;
    Evocation
Experiential learning, 143, 144, 200–201.
    See also Learning

F

Failure, 178–180. *See also* Mistakes
Families. *See also* Applications of MI;
    Practical applications of MI
    behavioral problems and, 78
    how MI might help with communicating
    with, 117–128
    overview, 116–117, 127
Fear about learning, 88–92. *See also*
    Learning
Feedback
    elicit–provide–elicit framework and,
        65–66
    learning MI and, 200, 203–204
    motivational interviewing in schools
    and, 8

Fighting behaviors, 79–86. *See also*
 Behavior
Financial aid process, 161
Focusing conversational pattern. *See also*
 Conversational patterns
 communication with parents or other
 family members and, 118, 119
 integrating MI in schools and, 198
 overview, 27, 29–30, 29*f*
Following style of communication. *See also*
 Communication styles
 behavioral problems and, 75, 75–76
 overview, 21
 personal growth and, 112, 115
Forward-looking summaries, 52, 53. *See*
 also Summarization

G

Giving advice and information. *See* Advice
 giving; Information, providing
Goal
 dropout prevention and, 149
 guiding style of communication and,
 22–23
 personal growth and, 109
 transitioning out of school and, 159
Grades, 121–124
Group counseling, 142
Guided Self-Change (GSC) program, 194
Guiding style of communication. *See also*
 Communication styles; Evocation
 autonomy, relatedness, and competence
 needs and, 64–65
 behavioral problems and, 75, 76
 communication with parents or other
 family members and, 120
 integrating MI in schools and, 194
 overview, 21, 21–23, 44–45
 personal growth and, 113, 114, 115

H

Home–school communication. *See* Families
Homework compliance, 92–97

I

Importance of change, 48–49. *See also*
 Change
Individual counseling, 142
Information, providing
 autonomy, relatedness, and competence
 needs and, 64–65
 communication with parents or other
 family members and, 120, 124
 elicit–provide–elicit framework and,
 63–66
 learning and, 88
 overview, 62–63, 67

In-school suspension, 156, 193
Institutes, 202–203
Instruction. *See* Teaching
Integrating MI in schools. *See also* Schools
 coaching and, 200, 203
 feedback and, 200, 203–204
 growing MI from within the school,
 195–197
 introducing MI, 199–200
 learning MI and, 199–204
 outside help, 192–195
 overview, 191–192
 professional development and, 197–199
Intervention, 141

J

Judgment
 behavioral problems and, 80
 communication with parents or other
 family members and, 118, 127
 compared to affirmation, 36
 learning MI and, 170–171, 172–173
 personal growth and, 107, 112
Jumping ahead, 56

K

Key question, 52, 53. *See also* Questioning

L

Labeling, 73–74, 140–141
Lateness, 75–78
Learning. *See also* Academic behavior;
 Applications of MI; At-risk students;
 Practical applications of MI; Teaching
 at-risk students and, 143, 144
 dropout prevention and, 152, 156
 how MI might help with, 88–100,
 107–110
 integrating MI in schools and, 197
 mistakes and, 59
 overview, 87–88, 101
 personal growth and, 103
Learning communities, 201–202. *See also*
 Professional development
Learning MI. *See also* Applications of MI;
 Motivational interviewing (MI) in
 general
 affirmation and, 178–180
 autonomy and, 186–188
 change talk and, 184–186
 exercises to practice, 188–190
 integrating MI in schools and, 199–204
 introducing MI, 199–200
 open questions and, 177–178
 overview, 169–171, 190
 reflection and, 180–182
 self-directed learning, 201

Learning MI (*continued*)
  spirit of MI and, 171–177
  summarization and, 182–184
Legal problems, 110–115, 147, 148
Limit setting, 75
Listening
  behavioral problems and, 83
  culturally diverse students and, 155
  empathy and, 34
  engagement and, 28–29
  learning MI and, 180–182
  motivational interviewing in schools
    and, 9
  overview, 39
  personal growth and, 103–104, 112
  reflection and, 37–40
  summarization and, 40–41

M

Math anxiety, 88–92
Mentorship, 196–197
Mind-sets, 144
Mistakes, 59, 178–180
Motivation. *See also* Change talk
  change and, 3, 5–6, 11–13
  dropout prevention and, 149, 151
  how MI might help with, 88–92
  learning and, 88
  learning MI and, 204
Motivational interviewing (MI) in general.
  See also Change talk; Integrating MI
  in schools; Learning MI; Practical
  applications of MI
  evoking and, 15–18
  foundations of, 13–15
  overview, 1, 3–4, 6–7, 11, 18–19, 69
  research literature on, 9–10
  schools and, 8–9
  spirit of MI, 23–26
Motivational Interviewing Network of
  Trainers (MINT), 202

N

Narrative therapy, 145
Needs. *See* Autonomy; Competence;
  Relatedness
Neutrality, 161–165
New Moves program, 194–195
Nonpunitive approaches, 143–145
Nonverbal cues, 89

O

OARS skills, 79–86. *See also* Affirmations;
  Core conversational skills; Open
  questions; Reflection; Summarization
Obesity, 194–195
Olweus Bullying Prevention Program
  (OBPP), 134

Open questions. *See also* Core
  conversational skills; OARS skills;
  Questioning
  behavioral problems and, 77, 80, 81
  bullying and, 136
  change talk and, 48, 50
  classwide discussions and, 98, 99–100
  communication with parents or other
    family members and, 118, 123
  dropout prevention and, 154
  learning and, 89, 90, 95
  learning MI and, 177–178
  motivational interviewing in schools
    and, 9
  overview, 17, 33, 34–36, 42
  personal growth and, 104–105, 106,
    108, 109
  transitioning out of school and, 165
Ownership, 57–58

P

Pace of a conversation, 34. *See also*
  Conversations
Parents. *See* Families
Participation, classroom, 8
Partnership
  communication with parents or other
    family members and, 117–128
  learning MI and, 172–173, 174
  personal growth and, 110–115
  spirit of MI and, 24, 25
Peer pressure, 103–107
Peer relationships. *See also* Bullying;
  Relationships
  dropout prevention and, 151
  how MI might help with, 103–107
  integrating MI in schools and, 196–197
  nonpunitive approaches and, 143
Permission
  advice giving and, 66
  behavioral problems and, 81
  communication with parents or other
    family members and, 124
  dropout prevention and, 153
  learning MI and, 188
  personal growth and, 105, 114
Personal development, 102, 103–115. *See
  also* Applications of MI; Practical
  applications of MI
Personal values card sort exercise,
  163–165. *See also* Values
Person-centered counseling style, 13
Perspective, 170–171
Persuasion, 12, 94
Planning. *See also* Planning conversational
  pattern
  evocation and, 54–57
  integrating MI in schools and, 199

learning and, 91
making a change plan, 57–60
overview, 54, 61
Planning conversational pattern, 27,
    31–32, 31f. *See also* Conversational
    patterns; Planning
Play, 143, 193
Postsecondary institutions, 159–165. *See
    also* Transition to life after school
Potential of a student, 107–110
Power, 132, 187–188
Practical applications of MI, 69–71. *See
    also* Applications of MI; Behavior;
    Families; Learning; Personal
    development
Praise, compared to affirmation, 36, 178
Preparatory change talk, 47. *See also*
    Change talk
Preparedness for class, 92–97
Pressure from peers, 103–107
Prevention efforts, 134
Principles of good practice, 140–142
Problem-solving skills
    behavioral problems and, 73
    dropout prevention and, 150–151, 152
    how MI might help with, 82–86
    integrating MI in schools and, 196
    personal growth and, 103
Professional development, 197–204
Project CHOICE, 194
Project Steps to Active Kids (STAK)
    program, 194–195
Punishment
    ambivalence and, 6
    at-risk students and, 140
    bullying and, 134–135, 137
    dropout prevention and, 151, 156

Q

Questioning. *See also* Open questions
    change talk and, 48–49, 52, 53
    communication with parents or other
        family members and, 120
    making a change plan and, 57–58
Questions, open. *See* Open questions

R

Rapid engagement, 28–29, 75–76. *See also*
    Engaging conversational pattern
Reaction, 67, 184
Readiness, 55–57, 61
Record-keeping of successes, 58–59, 61
Reengagement with school. *See also*
    Dropout prevention
    culturally diverse students and, 154–155
    how MI might help with, 150–156
    overview, 156–157
    research literature on, 148–150

Reflection. *See also* Core conversational
    skills; Listening; OARS skills
    behavioral problems and, 75–76, 77, 80,
        81, 82, 83, 84–85
    bullying and, 136–137, 138
    change talk and, 49–51, 53
    classwide discussions and, 97, 98, 99
    communication with parents or other
        family members and, 119, 120,
        122–123, 125, 126–128
    dropout prevention and, 152, 153–
        154
    empathy and, 34
    evoking and, 45
    learning and, 89, 90, 95, 96–97
    learning MI and, 172–173, 180–182
    overview, 33, 37–40, 42
    personal growth and, 103–104, 106,
        108, 109, 112, 113, 115
    planning and, 56, 61
    transitioning out of school and,
        164–165
Reflective listening. *See also* Listening;
    Reflection
    behavioral problems and, 83
    culturally diverse students and, 155
    learning and, 88
    learning MI and, 180–182
    overview, 17
Reinforcement, 58
Relatedness, 55, 64–65, 66–67
Relationships, 10, 103–107. *See also* Peer
    relationships; Relationships with
    students; Social problems
Relationships with students
    communication with parents or other
        family members and, 121–124
    dropout prevention and, 149–150,
        155–156
    giving information and advice and, 67
    reflection and, 40
    using MI to improve, 12
Research literature supporting MI, 9–10
Resistance, 5–6
Restorative justice, 143
Rewards
    ambivalence and, 6
    learning and, 93
    learning MI and, 204
Righting reflex
    ambivalence and, 5
    behavioral problems and, 75–76
    bullying and, 137–138
    learning and, 89, 94
    learning MI and, 175–177
    overview, 4–5
    personal growth and, 104, 105, 107
Rogers, Carl, 9

S

Scaffolding, 23
School–home communication. *See* Families
Schools, 8–9, 191–192. *See also* Integrating
    MI in schools
School-to-prison pipeline, 140
Schoolwide programs
    bullying and, 134
    integrating MI in schools and, 194–195,
        197
Self-awareness, 175
Self-confidence, 88–92, 110
Self-contained programs, 195–196
Self-determination theory, 55, 149
Self-directed learning, 201. *See also*
    Learning MI
Self-doubt, 88
Self-efficacy, 89, 141–142
Self-monitoring, 58–59, 61
Self-regulation
    at-risk students and, 141
    behavioral problems and, 73
    guiding style of communication and, 23
Seminars, 202–203
Sharing with others, 58–59, 61
Simple reflection, 40, 42. *See also*
    Reflection
Slips, 59
Social problems, 102, 103–115. *See also*
    Peer relationships; Relationships
Social–emotional skill development, 141
Socratic questioning, 23
Socratic style of education, 8
Solution focus, 104, 107
Special education, 140. *See also* At-risk
    students
Special needs students, 195–196
Specificity, 57
Spirit of MI, 20, 23–26, 32, 171–177
Staff, 197–199
Strengths. *See also* Affirmations
    affirming, 36
    communication with parents or other
        family members and, 119–120
    learning MI and, 184–186
    strengths-based approaches, 141–142
Students of color, 140. *See also* At-risk
    students; Cultural factors
Substance use, 194
Summaries, 17
Summarization. *See also* Core
    conversational skills; OARS skills
    behavioral problems and, 80
    change talk and, 52, 53
    classwide discussions and, 99
    evoking and, 45

learning and, 91
learning MI and, 182–184
overview, 33, 40–41, 42
personal growth and, 114
Sustain talk. *See also* Ambivalence; Change
    talk
    evocation and, 46–47, 53
    learning and, 89, 90, 94, 95, 96
    personal growth and, 108, 109
Sympathy, 33–34

T

Tardiness, 75–78
Teachers, 9, 197–199
Teacher–student relationships. *See*
    Relationships with students
Teaching. *See also* Learning
    Elicit–provide–elicit framework and, 65
    guiding style of communication and,
        22–23
    motivational interviewing in schools
        and, 8–9
    overview, 101
Telephone conversations with the family,
    116, 117–121. *See also* Families
Test results, 65–66
Transition to life after school. *See also*
    Applications of MI
    how MI might help with, 160–165
    neutrality and, 161–165
    overview, 158–160, 166
Transitions, 97–100
Truancy. *See also* Dropout prevention
    how MI might help with, 150–151
    overview, 146–148
    research literature on, 148

U

Uncertainty, 55–56
Understanding the material, 88–92
Understated reflections, 50–51, 188. *See
    also* Reflection
Unemployment, 159. *See also* Transition to
    life after school

V

Values, 103–107, 163–165

W

Well-being, 196
Whole-school MI integration. *See*
    Integrating MI in schools; Schoolwide
    programs
Workforce demands, 159–160. *See also*
    Transition to life after school
Workshops, 202–203